SNOT, SNEEZES, AND
SUPER-SPREADERS

First published in English by Greystone Books in 2022
Originally published in Dutch as *Viruswereld: Over snot en superspreaders*
in 2021 by Uitgeverij J.H. Gottmer/H.J.W. Becht BV, Haarlem, Netherlands;
a division of Gottmer Uitgeversgroep BV
Text copyright © 2021 by Marc ter Horst
Illustrations copyright © 2021 by Wendy Panders
English translation copyright © 2022 by Laura Watkinson
Foreword copyright © 2022 by Dr. Jennifer Gardy

22 23 24 25 26   5 4 3 2 1

Greystone Kids / Greystone Books Ltd.
greystonebooks.com

Cataloguing data available from Library and Archives Canada
ISBN 978-1-77164-973-5 (cloth)
ISBN 978-1-77164-974-2 (epub)

Editing by Linda Pruessen
Copy editing by Catherine Marjoribanks
Proofreading by Alison Strobel
Indexing by Stephen Ullstrom
Cover design by Wendy Panders and Belle Wuthrich
Interior design by Wendy Panders
Typesetting by Belle Wuthrich

Printed and bound in Singapore on FSC® certified paper at COS Printers Pte Ltd.
The FSC® label means that materials used for the product have been responsibly sourced.

Greystone Books gratefully acknowledges the Musqueam, Squamish, and
Tsleil-Waututh peoples on whose land our Vancouver head office is located.

Greystone Books thanks the Canada Council for the Arts, the British Columbia Arts Council,
the Province of British Columbia through the Book Publishing Tax Credit, and the Government
of Canada for supporting our publishing activities.

This publication has been made possible with financial support from
the Dutch Foundation for Literature.

Marc ter Horst

Illustrations by **Wendy Panders**

Foreword by **DR. JENNIFER GARDY**

Translated by **LAURA WATKINSON**

SNOT, SNEEZES AND SUPER-SPREADERS

Everything You Need to
Know About Viruses and
How to Stop Them

GREYSTONE KIDS

GREYSTONE BOOKS • VANCOUVER/BERKELEY/LONDON

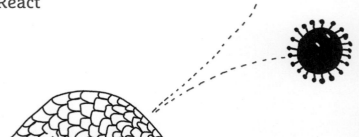

4 VIRUS STOPPERS
How to Frustrate a Virus

5 A FASCINATION WITH VACCINATION!
How Vaccines Protect Us

6 IN SEARCH OF THE SOURCE
How Virus Outbreaks Happen and What We Can Do About Them

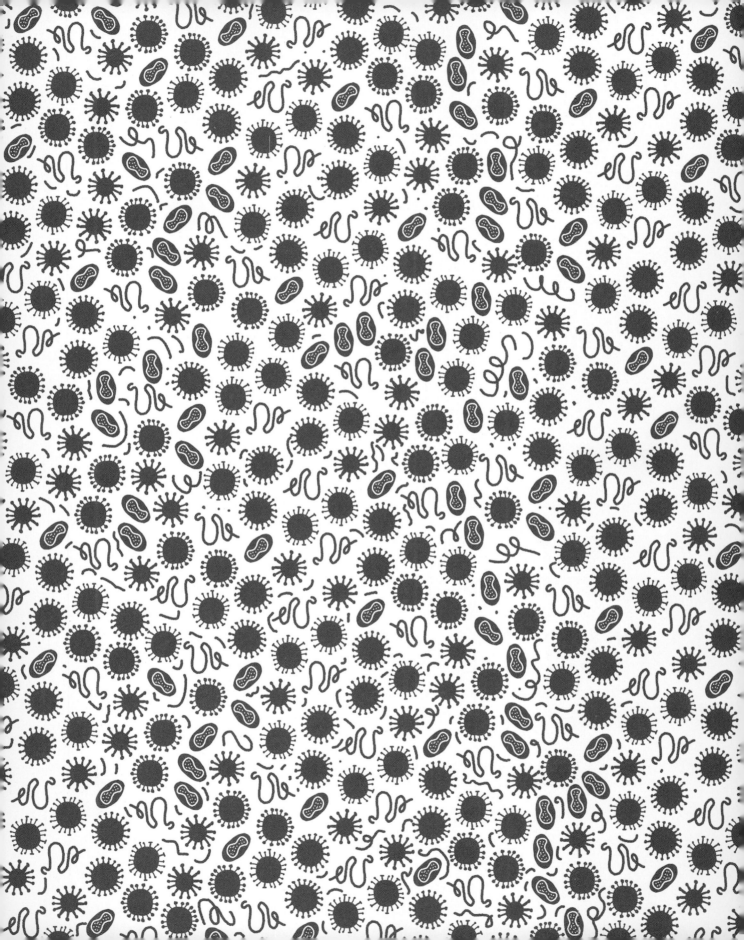

Dear readers,

When I was young, I was given a very special book—one a lot like the book you're holding in your hands right now. It told the story of the famous scientist Louis Pasteur. I won't give too much away because you'll be meeting Pasteur in these pages very soon, but here's a sneak preview—he was one of the first people to figure out that tiny, almost invisible microorganisms like bacteria and viruses could make people sick.

To me, this was the most interesting thing I'd ever heard! Finally! An explanation for why sometimes I'd get sniffles or a cough or funny spots—it was a germ! A germ I couldn't see, multiplying inside my body and causing my immune system to do all sorts of unusual things. What a strange and fascinating idea!

From that day onwards, I was obsessed with microbes. I wanted to learn anything and everything I could about the bacteria, viruses, parasites, and fungi that make people sick. I read books, I watched films, and eventually I went to university to study infectious diseases.

And now, many decades after I first learned about the incredible world of germs, I get to study them every day. My work as a disease detective has taken me around the world, from talking about tracking outbreaks at the World Health Organization in Geneva to sequencing virus DNA in a laboratory in Ghana. And the more I learn, the more I realize how much we still have to discover about the incredible world of viruses.

I hope that this book is the beginning of your fascination with these marvelous microbes! So turn the page, and prepare to enter a universe of snot, sneezes, and super-spreaders . . . a universe of viruses!

—Dr. Jennifer Gardy, infectious disease scientist and educator

NASTY TO MEET YOU

Welcome to the mysterious world of viruses! There are millions of them, they are everywhere, and they're so small that you've never seen one. And yet they have a huge impact on our lives. Just look at COVID-19. Hopefully, by the time you read this, the COVID-19 virus will be nothing more than an annoying nuisance (and one seriously bad memory!). But how did this unwanted guest come into our lives in the first place? To refresh your memory, I'll take you back to the strange events of the year 2020.

After that you can discover...
• how many viruses there are inside you
• how big you'd need to be to jump over Mount Everest
• which cheese contains little creatures
• which virus looks really ridiculous
• why your earlobes are the shape they are
• what the advantage of looking different is
• how long it takes to count to a billion

In short: What viruses are and how they work.

ONE YEAR OF COVID-19

December 20, 2019
In Canada, children are about to have their Christmas break. The teacher clears her desk and makes sure the tape over her webcam is still firmly in place. "What's the point of that thing, anyway?" she thinks.

In Australia, bushfires break out. In China, the markets that sell live animals are busy. In the United States, Post Malone is googling to see which country is hosting the Pinkpop music festival. People in Europe can't wait for the annual Eurovision Song Contest. And everywhere, top health officials can still go out in public without being recognized.

December 26, 2019
It's the day after Christmas, and around the world lots of children are visiting their grandmas and grandpas. In England, the soccer stadiums are full. In India, hundreds of public places are packed with people watching the solar eclipse. In China, an elderly couple arrives at the hospital in Wuhan. The man and woman are tired, feverish, and having trouble breathing. Dr. Zhang Jixian thinks it could be flu or pneumonia. To be on the safe side, she arranges for a CAT scan to be done: a computer photograph of the inside of the body that's made by putting the patient on a narrow table and sliding them into a big white ring.

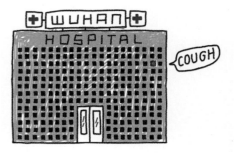

December 27, 2019
In the photographs, Zhang Jixian sees gray patches on the patients' lungs. That's suspicious. She asks the couple's son to have a CAT scan too—and he has the same patches on his lungs. This seems to suggest an infectious disease. That day, another new patient arrives at the hospital, a trader from the live-animal market in Wuhan. Zhang Jixian keeps these patients separate from the rest of the hospital. They go into quarantine. If this is a new virus, she can't take any risks, because most people have no protection against new viruses.

January 6, 2020
In Canada and the United States, the winter break is over and the children go back to school. They give their teachers high fives as they enter the classroom. They use their hands to wipe their runny noses but then spend less than three seconds when they wash up in the bathroom. The live-animal market in Wuhan is shut down.

January 23, 2020

By this point, 581 infections and 17 deaths have been recorded. Wuhan and the surrounding area go into lockdown. Airports, highways, and railroads are closed. Hardly anyone is allowed to enter or leave the area. Roughly 60 million people are in quarantine, for at least two months. "They left it a bit late," say some world experts, because in the past month around 5 million residents have already traveled by train or plane to other cities in China. And to countries all over the globe.

February 11, 2020

By now, the virus has turned up in other countries, including Thailand, Australia, Russia, Italy, Belgium, Canada, and the United States. Worldwide, more than 43,000 cases have been recorded, and at least 1,000 people have died of the virus.

The World Health Organization names the new virus SARS-CoV-2 and the sickness COVID-19, after the year when it was discovered. You might know the virus better as "coronavirus" and the sickness as "COVID," so that's what I'll call them in the rest of this book. But here's an important fact: SARS-CoV-2 isn't the only coronavirus.

February 27, 2020

In Italy, the number of patients is rapidly rising. In the Netherlands, the first coronavirus patient reports to the hospital in Tilburg: he went skiing in northern Italy before taking part in a street festival to celebrate Carnival in the Dutch province of Brabant.

In Canada, provincial leaders are arguing about whether people should be advised to stockpile essentials "in case of emergency." And two days later, on February 29, the United States will report its first confirmed coronavirus death.

March 11, 2020

There are now 118,319 infections in total, spread over 113 countries. Worldwide, at least 4,292 people have died of the virus. The World Health Organization officially declares the virus outbreak a pandemic. That means it's an infectious disease that's spread across much of the world.

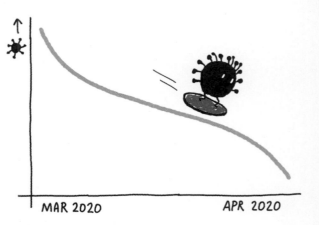

March 14, 2020

France and Spain order all restaurants to close, and everywhere people are advised to stay home as much as possible, to avoid infecting one another.

A few days earlier the NBA and the NHL suspended their seasons. And soon the Pinkpop music festival, the UEFA soccer tournament, and the Eurovision Song Contest will be canceled as well.

March 25, 2020

Many parts of the world are now in lockdown. Out on the streets, it's quiet. There are pictures on TV of a Spanish emergency hospital with 1,350 patients. In the newspapers, there are scary stories about Italian hospitals where the patients have to lie in the hallway. The United States officially leads the world in COVID cases, with at least 81,321 confirmed infections and more than 1,000 deaths. Visits to long-term care facilities are restricted, and some children lose their elderly loved ones without being able to say goodbye.

But there are also positive stories, about people helping one another. They buy groceries for the doctors and nurses who are working so hard. Musicians play in the gardens of nursing homes for lonely residents. Teddy bears appear in windows, so children can have fun spotting them when they're out for a walk.

April 5, 2020

From the beginning of April, in many countries, fewer and fewer patients report to the hospital. Intensive Care Units (ICUs) are slowly becoming quieter too. The lockdowns are working. This becomes clear about two weeks after the introduction of the stricter measures, as it can take up to two weeks to find out that someone has been infected.

May 11, 2020

After months of learning at home, with online help from teachers, children in some places, like the Netherlands, are now going back to school. They're wearing masks and skipping the high fives, though. In North America, most students will have to wait till the next school year to see their teachers in person.

July 4, 2020

The World Health Organization reports a record number of infections: 212,326 in one day. The situation in Brazil, India, and the United States is particularly serious. But some European nations appear to be weathering the storm reasonably well, and where the numbers of cases are low, some lucky people are even able to go to hairdressers and barbers again!

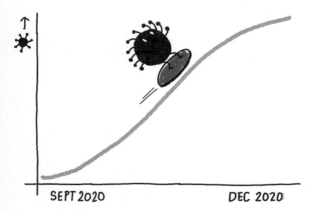

SEPT 2020   DEC 2020

September 28, 2020

Worldwide, 1 million people have died of the coronavirus. And in some places where the case numbers were low and people were starting to feel lucky, they are beginning to climb again, in what the scientists are calling the start of the "second wave." North American children are back at school, but will they be stuck at home again soon? And what will the winter holidays look like this year?

November 9, 2020

Good news: It's announced that the first fully tested vaccine offers incredible protection, reducing people's risk of getting infected by over 90 percent. In Russia and China people have been receiving vaccines for some time, but none that have been this thoroughly tested. Europe will get the new vaccine in December. Before the end of the year the U.S. Food and Drug Administration (FDA) will give a vaccine "Emergency Use Authorization" for Americans, and Health Canada will approve a vaccine for Canadians, too.

December 26, 2021

Two years after the first patients were hospitalized in Wuhan, the good news is that 8.55 billion doses of vaccine have been distributed, and over 56 percent of the world's population has received at least one vaccine shot, with many people lining up for a third. But the virus continues to mutate and take different forms, and this time it's the turn of the omicron variant to be the big bully. What could be next?

DON'T BE SCARED

There's a virus on your nose! And on your fingertip, too. And in your tummy. In your lungs, in your brain. On the table. On the corner of this page. On the dot at the end of this sentence. In the air you're breathing in. In the water you drink. They really are absolutely everywhere. On the tops of mountains, deep in the oceans, and high in the sky. Viruses, viruses, viruses. There are countless different types of virus, and all of them are made up of millions and millions and millions of virus particles.

Should you be scared of them? Of course not! You, and every other human being, have been living with these viruses all your life. You breathe them in, drink them down, poop them out. And, your whole life long, it's been going fine. Well, apart from that time you had that bad cold, and those few days with a stomach bug. But those really are the exceptions. Because the truth is that almost all the viruses that hang around with us are pretty harmless. And some of them are actually really useful. For example—viruses do a great job of fighting against bacteria, as you're about to see.

There are thousands of species of virus on and in your body, and every virus has its own favorite spot. You know that moles live in the ground, squirrels live up in the trees, deer live in the woods—that's their habitat. Well, in the same way, your body is a sort of habitat for viruses. One virus loves living inside your tummy. Another virus is thrilled to make its home between your teeth. And another one likes lazing around in a bed of boogers up your nose.

There's obviously no need to be scared of them. The forest isn't scared of the animals who live there either. In fact, the animals help the forest. If the squirrel didn't hide so many acorns, there wouldn't be so many trees. All the animals and plants work together to keep the forest healthy. It only becomes unhealthy when there are way too many or way too few of a particular species. Or when a new species comes wandering into the forest and throws off the balance of life.

So, most of the viruses on and in your body are perfectly fine. Your body is used to them. In fact, some them are even helpful, doing various tasks that keep you healthy. It's the new viruses that can be the harmful ones—because your body doesn't know them yet. Or new versions of existing viruses. If you ingest the norovirus, you can expect a few days of severe diarrhea. The cold virus will give you a runny nose and a cough—it's also a type of coronavirus. And the new version of the coronavirus that we're dealing with now can give you COVID. It doesn't make everyone sick, but everyone needs to be careful. And it can certainly be dangerous for older people, and people who have other health problems.

1 centimeter = 10 millimeters

1 micrometer = 0.001 millimeters

1 nanometer = 0.000001 millimeters

IT'S A SMALL WORLD

One little drop of seawater contains 10 million virus particles. Not exactly, of course. It could be a few more or less. But that should give you an idea how tiny virus particles are. The world of viruses is a very small world indeed.

The size of a virus particle isn't usually measured in fractions of inches or centimeters or millimeters. Luckily, scientists have come up with smaller units, like micrometers and nanometers. Personally, I think a millimeter is already pretty tiny. That's about the size of a small head louse. If you've ever had head lice, you know how hard they are to spot. And if you've never seen a head louse, hold five pages of this book between your fingers. The thickness of those five pages together is about a millimeter.

A micrometer is a thousand times smaller than a millimeter. So, it's completely invisible. A hair is about 100 micrometers thick. The largest human cell can also be measured in micrometers: the ovum, the egg cell where your life began, was about 100 to 200 micrometers in size. It is *just* possible to see one of those without a microscope. Your dad's sperm cell, which fertilized the egg, was a lot smaller: it had a head of 4 micrometers and a tail of 50 micrometers. A bacterium is even smaller than that: about 1 to 5 micrometers. But that's giant compared to a virus particle.

We measure viruses in nanometers. A nanometer is a thousand times smaller than a micrometer. That makes it a million times smaller than a millimeter. So, a head louse is 1 million nanometers in size. And the smallest bacterium is 1,000 nanometers. But a virus particle is somewhere between 20 and 300 nanometers. You want to know something that's even smaller? DNA, the building code that lives inside each of our cells, is a package 2 nanometers in size. But if you unwrap that package, you get a string that's 6 feet (2 meters) long. That's pretty impressive!

Let's look at it a different way. Imagine you could magnify the flu virus ten thousand times. Then it would be 1 millimeter in size, the size of a head louse. So, compared to a magnified virus, a head louse would be the size of a stegosaurus. And a stegosaurus would be the size of Canada's Prince Edward Island. And you? You would be big enough to jump over Mount Everest, the highest mountain on Earth.

So, you can understand why viruses can't be seen with the naked eye. They can't even be seen with an ordinary microscope. The question is . . . how do we know they exist?

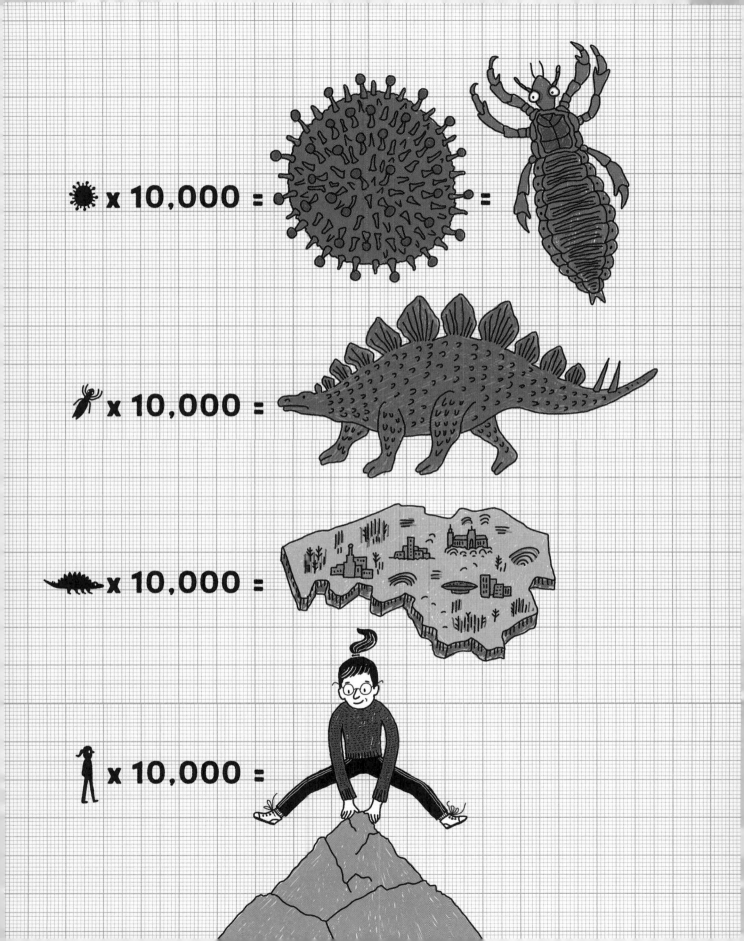

x 10,000 = =

x 10,000 =

x 10,000 =

x 10,000 =

ANTONIE van LEEUWENHOEK

ZOOMING IN

In France, they use little animals to make cheese. It's true! These creatures are called cheese mites, and they give the cheese a special flavor by making tiny tunnels in the crust. The cheese mite is a sort of spider that grows no larger than 1/64th of an inch (0.5 millimeters). That's half the size of the tiny head louse we were talking about. In the seventeenth century, scientists believed the cheese mite was the smallest living creature on Earth. But then the Dutch scientist Antonie van Leeuwenhoek got involved. His hobby was making lenses—and being curious about things. He used his lenses to make microscopes that could magnify objects by up to three hundred times. Then he used his microscopes to look more closely at all kinds of objects: a drop of blood, a splash of water from a well, a dash of saliva from his mouth. And that was how Van Leeuwenhoek became the first person to see bacteria. Since he wasn't yet sure what they were, he decided to call them "little animals."

Two centuries later, it became clear that bacteria cause a lot of illnesses. At that time, there was a disease that was killing tobacco plants. Their leaves faded, the plants withered, and sometimes entire harvests failed. The Dutch biologist Martinus Willem Beijerinck carried out research into the disease. He took some infected leaves, made them into a paste, and then passed the paste through a filter with holes so small that no bacteria could go through it. What was left was a liquid without bacteria, which he smeared onto healthy tobacco plants. He reasoned that if the disease was really caused by bacteria, these plants would not become sick. You guessed it: the plants became sick anyway. That meant bacteria were not to blame.

MARTINUS WILLEM BEIJERINCK

ERNST RUSKA

Next, Beijerinck put the sap of these plants into the filter too. If the disease was caused by a toxin in the sap, then filtering it would make the poison weaker. But that didn't happen. So, apparently, whatever was causing the disease was reproducing within the plant. Beijerinck had discovered something that was much smaller than a bacterium: a virus. Some people call him the founder of virology, which is the study of viruses. But there were also researchers in Russia and other parts of the world who discovered viruses at around the same time.

Beijerinck was never able to see the virus particles with his own eyes. Back in his day, there were only ordinary microscopes that were not very powerful. They worked using light—a lot like the microscopes you have at school. As the wavelength of light is larger than the largest virus particle, you can't use a microscope like that to see viruses. It's complicated, but it basically means that viruses can slip unseen through the waves of light. It's a bit like hunting tadpoles with a shark net.

In 1931, the German physicist Ernst Ruska built the first electron microscope. Instead of light particles, this kind of microscope uses a different kind of particle to make the small world visible: electrons. If you accelerate electrons, they have a much smaller wavelength than light. So, you can use them to see much smaller things. For the first time, scientists were able to look at viruses. The images were still a bit blurry, but nowadays the latest technology allows us to see details of 0.05 nanometers. If a virus particle had a mouth, you'd be able to see it laughing.

SPOT THE DIFFERENCE

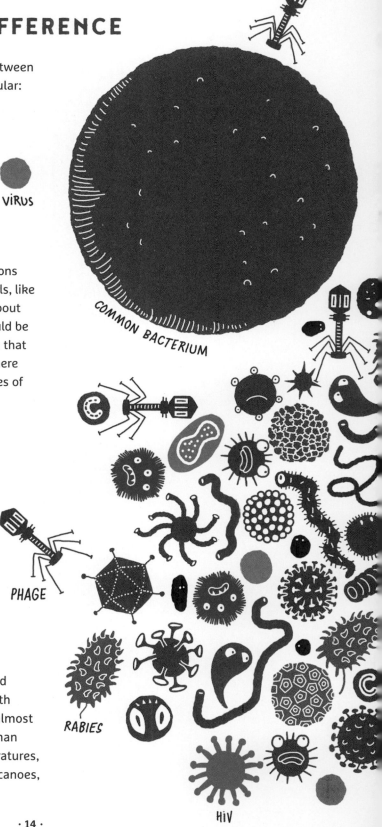

Lots of people don't know the difference between a virus and a bacterium (that's the singular: one bacterium, many bacteria). Which is a bit like not being able to tell the difference between a mushroom and a giraffe. To be fair, though, viruses and bacteria are kind of similar. They're both so small that you can't see them with the naked eye. But most viruses are between ten and a hundred times smaller than the average bacterium.

There are millions of species of viruses and billions of species of bacteria. Compare that to mammals, like dolphins, mice, and human beings. There are about 6,500 different known mammals, and there could be hundreds more that are so small or well hidden that they have yet to be discovered. All told, then, there are more than a thousand times as many species of viruses and bacteria as there are of mammals.

All those viruses and bacteria look very different. Some are really dull, and others are totally wild. They come in the form of balls, rods, spirals, with and without tails, hair, or spikes. And then there's a virus called the bacteriophage—but you can call it phage. The phage is a virus with a really wacky appearance—it looks like it might land on the moon at any moment and start doing research. In fact, it hunts and destroys bacteria. So, you can thank it for keeping the number of bacteria on Earth—and inside your body—under control.

In nearly every corner of the world, bacteria and viruses are fighting an endless war. They're both found in the strangest places on Earth and in almost every part of your body. Bacteria are tougher than viruses, though. Viruses don't like high temperatures, but bacteria can even live near underwater volcanoes,

VIRUS

COMMON BACTERIUM

PHAGE

RABIES

HIV

CORONAVIRUS

EBOLA

SARS

SMALLPOX

NOROVIRUS

1918 FLU

where it's hotter than 212 degrees Fahrenheit (100 degrees Celsius). Viruses can't exist outside a living body for long, but the only thing bacteria need to reproduce endlessly is a dishcloth.

You already know that most viruses are completely harmless—or even useful. The same can be said for bacteria. But some viruses and bacteria can make you really sick. And because they're so small, it's easy for them to spread. Viruses and bacteria are launched by a sneeze, hitch a ride on poop, or hang around on a doorknob. Before you know it, they've infected their next victim. If those infections happen much faster than normal within a particular area, it's called an epidemic. And when the epidemic spreads farther, spanning many countries or even continents, we call it a pandemic. That's why the World Health Organization declared the coronavirus epidemic a pandemic.

Of course, not all diseases are equally bad. For instance, I know for a fact that you've been infected by viruses and bacteria dozens of times. Sometimes you didn't even notice. Sometimes you had to stay in bed for a few days. But hey, you're still here. Sick-nesses like flu and impetigo aren't a big problem for most children. However, the same diseases can really make some people very sick, and there are some diseases that are even more serious.

You've probably had the flu before. It's a virus that usually gives you a fever, a sore throat, and aching muscles. It's way more annoying than a cold. Impetigo is caused by bacteria and gives you itchy bumps that you should try not to scratch. That's another difference—some diseases are caused by viruses and some by bacteria. COVID, flu, and smallpox are examples of diseases caused by viruses. Cholera, impetigo, and the Plague are caused by bacteria. But now for the biggest and weirdest difference...

DEAD OR ALIVE

Humans are alive. Robots are not. Jellyfish are alive. Water is not. Cactuses are alive. Canned peaches are not. And what about viruses? Are they alive? Not everyone agrees on that subject. It depends on how you define life. Usually, we consider something to be alive when it reacts to its surroundings, when it takes care of providing its own energy, and when it can reproduce. It doesn't matter how. Using flowers and bees, as plants do. Or through sex, as humans do. Or simply by splitting yourself in two—that's how bacteria do it. So, bacteria are living creatures. And so are your parents.

But viruses—that's a different story. They are incredibly lazy layabouts. They can't do very much without outside help. They can reproduce only by hijacking someone else's cell and converting it into a copying machine. Viruses don't have any cells themselves. And that's a sign that they're not really alive, because cells are the building blocks of all living things. Your body, for example, is made up of more than 20 trillion cells. That's 20 million times a million. And you can double that number if you also count the 20 trillion bacteria in your body. Because every bacterium is made of precisely one single cell.

More complicated creatures, like you, have all kinds of cells: skin cells, nerve cells, brain cells. Together, those cells form your body. And inside every cell, there's a code that dictates everything about your body and your character. That code is called DNA, and it's the same in all your cells. But what's in *your* cells is different from what's in my cells, in your grandma's cells, or in the cells of a duck-billed platypus. That's why the police use DNA to expose criminals. If detectives find blood or hair at a crime scene, they can investigate whether the DNA in the hair or blood cells is a match for the suspect's DNA.

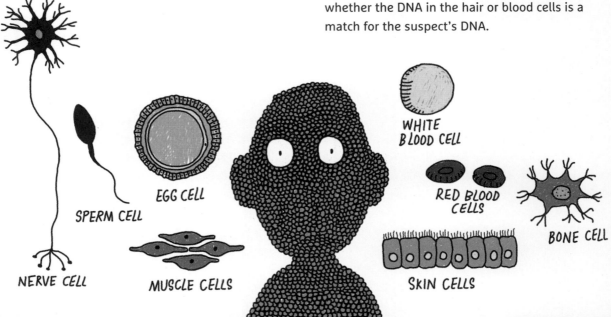

NERVE CELL

SPERM CELL

EGG CELL

MUSCLE CELLS

WHITE BLOOD CELL

RED BLOOD CELLS

BONE CELL

SKIN CELLS

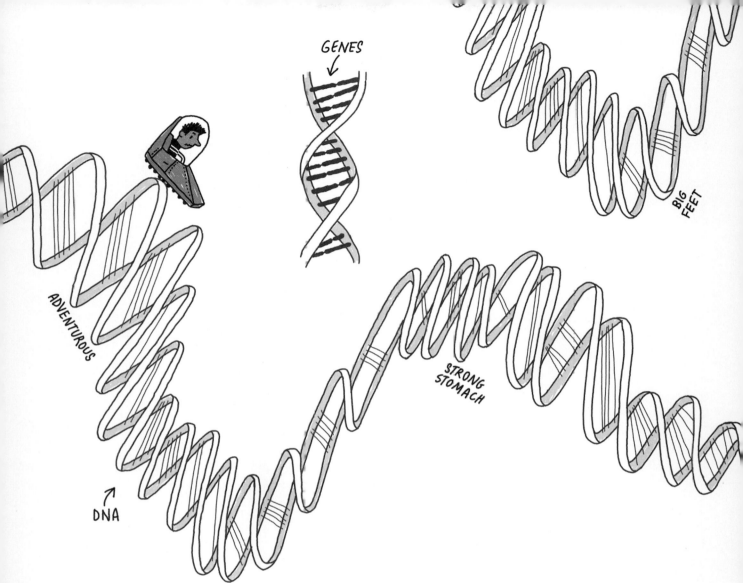

GENES

BIG
FEET

ADVENTUROUS

STRONG
STOMACH

DNA

DNA twists around and looks like an endless roller coaster that would make you feel really sick. And each piece in a strand of DNA has information about one of your characteristics. These pieces are called genes, and humans have around 21,000 of them. There's a gene for the color of your eyes, a gene for the shape of your earlobes, and a gene for how quickly you get angry. A plant doesn't have those particular genes, but it does have DNA that you don't, such as a gene for the shape of its leaves and a gene for the length of its roots. Viruses also have DNA, or a code that's similar: RNA. But because viruses aren't made up of cells, that code simply floats around inside them. In fact, a virus

is in the genes. And this is important information because the shape of the virus also determines which cells it can enter. These can be the cells of humans, animals, plants, or bacteria.

Once a virus is inside a cell, the virus reveals its code. This is a complete recipe for making new viruses. The virus actually uses the cell as a copying machine. The code says, "Copy me! Copy me!" And that's what the cell does. It helps the virus to reproduce. But, just like the photocopier at school, sometimes it can get a bit messed up. And I'm not talking about paper jams or empty ink cartridges. These are copying errors that cost lives.

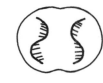

COPYING ERRORS

Take a good look at your body. It's made up of trillions of cells. And most of the cells that now form your body weren't there a few years ago. That's because your cells are constantly being replaced. And yet you are still entirely yourself—because each cell contains your unique genes and passes them on to the new cells. First, the DNA in the cell is split in two, like unzipping a zipper. One half stays behind in the old cell, and the other half goes into the new one. But that can only happen, of course, when they both zip together to form a complete roller coaster again. So, both halves are reconstructed until they're whole. Now the cell, complete with DNA, can be copied.

This is an incredibly complicated process. Do the math. If DNA were a book, it would contain 3 billion letters. That's over 1,000 times the length of the Bible, or 20,000 times all the letters in this book. And every time the cell divides, those letters have to be copied. The cell does this really quickly, in just a few hours. So, it's no wonder that a mistake sneaks in now and then. That's called a mutation. The more often a cell divides, the more mutations there are. And parents pass those mutations on to their children. Usually this has hardly any consequences at all. But sometimes a mutation turns out to be very useful.

Picture a valley full of hares. Most of the hares are brown. This means they don't stand out in a valley. That's important because the hares are constantly battling for survival. They're always searching for food, while also trying to avoid becoming food for a predator. Animals who are successful at that stand more chance of staying alive. A hare with strong legs and a good camouflage color will probably have a longer life than his distant cousin with a limp and a tuft of orange fur on his head. The animals that live longer stand more chance of having babies. And because those babies are like their parents, they also have the same useful qualities, which gives them more chance of surviving and having even more babies.

Year after year, the hares continue to reproduce. Most hares are like their parents, but because of a copying error in the DNA (a mutation), there are also a few with lighter fur. It gradually becomes colder in the valley. Snow falls more often, so the brown hares are now easier for birds of prey to spot. Now their brown fur is no longer an advantage. The hares with lighter fur have a greater chance of survival. They have baby hares who also have light coats. So, more and more hares in the valley end up with light coats.

The same happens with other characteristics. Hares with thicker fur are nice and warm in the snow. Hares with slightly smaller ears hold on to their warmth for longer. The brown hares with thin fur and large ears have a hard time. They often get eaten before they can have babies. The white hares are better suited to life in the new situation and are more likely to survive. This goes on for thousands of years. Thanks to a copying error, a new species emerges: the arctic hare. They are white, with thick fur and small ears.

Unfortunately, with viruses, the copying errors are sometimes a little less cute.

FROM ANIMAL TO HUMAN

I have a number in my head between one and a billion. Guess what it is. What did you say? Sorry! Wrong! You lose! Well, you only had one chance in a billion to get it right. That's how it works with mutations, too. Hardly any mutations result in advantages. There were millions of mutations in the hare DNA that didn't help the hares at all. And then there was the hare with the lighter coat.

But viruses are much better at mutating than hares and other animals. This is because they might be lazy and sloppy, but they reproduce at lightning speed. When you have a cold, you turn into a little virus factory that's like a 3D printer producing millions of virus particles. Every virus particle contains small mistakes. Usually, those mistakes are a disadvantage or make no difference. But the more virus particles copy themselves, the more chance there is that a mutation will come along that's beneficial for the virus. That advantage will allow the virus to copy itself more often, and more

of those virus particles will come along, and so on. It's as if the virus is able to say all the numbers from one to a billion at the same time. Which would take you about a hundred years, without a break.

That's how it works with animal viruses. You have thousands of viruses in your body, which usually don't bother you much. And animals have their own viruses that do them no harm at all. They just lie there snoozing away inside a turkey's beak or a bat's stomach—and copying themselves, with all the usual errors. The result is millions of virus particles that differ slightly from one another. Most of these mistakes don't make much difference. But occasionally there's a mutation that could prove very useful. For example, a spike with a shape that's just a little bit different, which coincidentally turns out to be the key to entering a human cell. Then all the virus has to do is meet a human and make the jump.

This "jumping" isn't actual jumping, of course. That's just what people say when a virus moves from an animal to a human. A virus doesn't have any legs to jump with. It lies around, just being there. But because there are so many viruses,

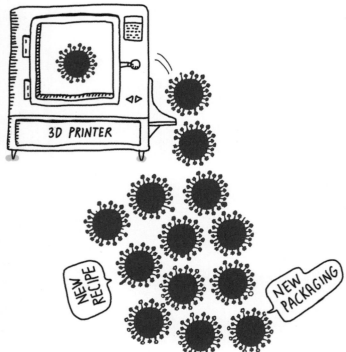

and because they're so incredibly tiny, it sometimes happens that a mutated animal virus finds its way into a human cell. Then you get a new virus that humans aren't used to, and to which they have no resistance. Like the coronavirus that

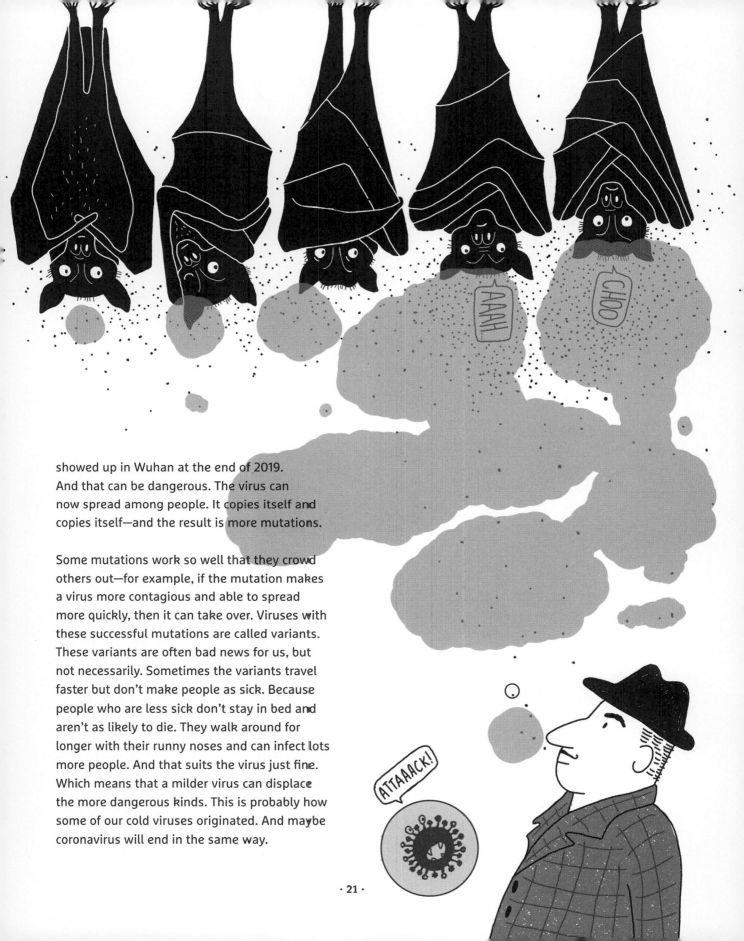

showed up in Wuhan at the end of 2019.
And that can be dangerous. The virus can
now spread among people. It copies itself and
copies itself—and the result is more mutations.

Some mutations work so well that they crowd
others out—for example, if the mutation makes
a virus more contagious and able to spread
more quickly, then it can take over. Viruses with
these successful mutations are called variants.
These variants are often bad news for us, but
not necessarily. Sometimes the variants travel
faster but don't make people as sick. Because
people who are less sick don't stay in bed and
aren't as likely to die. They walk around for
longer with their runny noses and can infect lots
more people. And that suits the virus just fine.
Which means that a milder virus can displace
the more dangerous kinds. This is probably how
some of our cold viruses originated. And maybe
coronavirus will end in the same way.

· 21 ·

SNOT AND SUPER-SPREADERS

Viruses have all kinds of sneaky ways of spreading. And they can't do it without us. Take the SARS virus that appeared in Asia in 2003. One day, it just hopped onto a plane. It didn't buy a ticket, but it did go through security. The Virus Story is about this round-the-world trip.

After that you can discover…
• why viruses think everything was worse in the old days
• how to reach half of humanity with just two followers
• what kind of clouds you can't see
• why you should never pet stray dogs
• whose peaches and ice cream you shouldn't eat
• a good excuse for buying M&M's

In short: How viruses spread.

VIRUS STORY

ROOM 911

More than 9,000 miles (15,000 kilometers) separate the big cities of Singapore and Toronto. However, the same mysterious disease appeared in those two places almost simultaneously. And not just there. At the end of February 2003, people in Hong Kong, Hanoi, and Vancouver also reported that they were suffering from a strange new disease.

The doctors had a puzzle on their hands. The patients were feverish, short of breath, and nauseated. All the symptoms indicated pneumonia, but the usual medication didn't work. The doctors thought it could be a new disease. So, it seemed like a good idea to isolate the patients: they were each given their own room, and anyone who came into contact with them had to wear protective clothing and face masks. By the time they did this, though, hospital workers were getting sick as well. And members of the patients' families were taken to the hospital too, feeling desperately ill. There was still a lot of uncertainty about the new disease, but everyone could tell that it was pretty infectious. So, it was important to find the source of the infection. Did the woman from Toronto infect the woman from Singapore? Or was it the other way around? Or had they both caught it from the same source? Sometimes virology is just like detective work.

The patient from Singapore was called Esther Mok. Her doctor spoke with doctors at other city hospitals every week, and he told them about Esther Mok's mysterious illness. It immediately

ESTHER MOK

caught the attention of another doctor. "That's a coincidence. There's a young woman in our hospital with the same symptoms!" It turned out to be Esther Mok's friend. They'd just spent a weekend shopping together in Hong Kong. Had one of them infected the other? Or had they both caught the disease in Hong Kong? Because there had been another case there. And that person had stayed at the same hotel as Esther and her friend. All three stayed on the ninth floor of the Hotel Metropole. Three guesses who also stayed there at the same time—the woman from Toronto. And I might as well tell you right away: the patients from Hanoi and Vancouver and a few others had been staying on the ninth floor of the Hotel Metropole in Hong Kong at the same time too.

Mystery solved? Hmm, not entirely. Which one of the hotel guests had infected the others? Who was the source?

To work that out, you could take a look at which guests got sick, which nights they stayed at the hotel, and in which rooms. Esther Mok and her friend stayed in room 938. The woman from Toronto was in room 904. And there were twelve other hotel guests who ended up in the hospital.

LIU JIANLUN

The first one to go to the hospital was the guest from room 911. On February 22, 2003, he left the hotel, feeling really sick, and staggered to a hospital around the corner from the Hotel Metropole. He was Liu Jianlun, a sixty-four-year-old doctor and medical professor from Guangzhou. The day before, February 21, 2003, he and his wife had taken the bus from Guangzhou to Hong Kong. He'd been suffering flu symptoms for the past few days, but he'd recovered enough to go to his nephew's wedding. At least, he thought he had.

After a bus ride of three hours, the couple arrived in Hong Kong. They had something to eat, went shopping, and checked in at the Hotel Metropole. Where it turned out that he didn't feel so good after all. Coughing away, he dragged himself to their room. Some researchers believe he also vomited on the carpet in the hallway.

The couple never got to the nephew's wedding. The following day, they checked out of the hotel and the professor reported to the nearby hospital, short of breath and with a high fever. He warned the doctors that he was afraid he had an infectious disease. After all, he was a doctor himself, at the hospital in Guangzhou, where dozens of hospital employees had recently reported sick

after a local seafood merchant, Zhou Zuofeng, had been admitted with a mysterious disease that resembled pneumonia. They probably became infected because he was coughing and sputtering when they gave him oxygen to help him with his breathing.

Professor Liu Jianlun died on March 4, 2003. By that point, the other guests on the ninth floor had left. With the infectious virus inside their bodies, they boarded planes to Singapore, Toronto, and other big cities. They probably never even spoke to the professor. Maybe they briefly rode the elevator together, where they might have pressed the same button. And they certainly walked on the same ugly carpet in the hallway. Somehow or other, they caught the disease. Although no one knew yet what disease it was. Research was needed—and that research would cost an Italian doctor his life.

JOHNNY CHEN

Johnny Chen, an American businessman, was staying at the Hotel Metropole at the same time as Professor Liu Jianlun. His room was 910, across the hallway from room 911. Right after flying to Vietnam, he was admitted to the hospital in Hanoi. The hospital called in the help of Carlo Urbani, an Italian doctor from the World Health Organization (WHO), who was stationed in Hanoi at the time. Urbani examined Johnny Chen and soon realized this was a new and highly infectious lung disease. He immediately raised the alarm and informed the WHO. The WHO alerted hospitals all over the world to keep an eye out and to take appropriate measures if necessary.

In Singapore, schools closed. Whole neighborhoods in Toronto went into quarantine. Airplanes were grounded. Carlo Urbani's quick

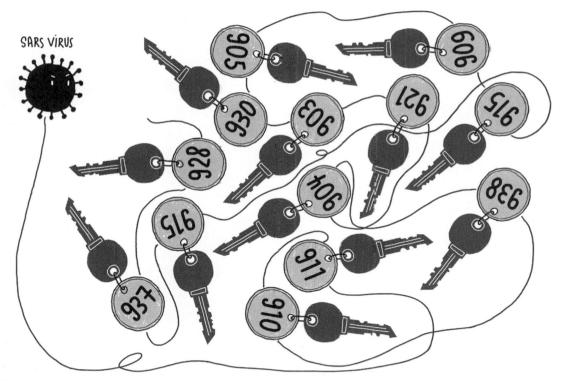

SARS VIRUS

CARLO URBANI

action probably saved thousands of lives. However, Urbani himself died of the disease on March 29, 2003. It was not clear at that point that a virus was involved, but they'd already come up with a name for the disease: SARS, or Severe Acute Respiratory Syndrome.

On April 16, 2003, it was announced that the cause of the disease was a totally new virus. And it was a mutation of that same virus that brought more than half the world to its knees in 2020 and 2021. SARS was the forerunner of that coronavirus.

On July 5, 2003, the WHO declared that the SARS outbreak was under control. Six months later, there were a few more cases in China, but they were quickly recognized, so they didn't result in an epidemic. In total, 8,098 people in 26 countries became infected with the SARS virus, and 774 died. It could have been roughly half that number if Professor Liu Jianlun had not gone to Hong Kong. And even less if Zhou Zuofeng, the seafood merchant from Guangzhou, hadn't visited Zhongshan at the beginning of 2003. It's most likely that the virus made the jump from animals to humans in Zhongshan a couple of months earlier, and that Zhou Zuofeng came into contact there with one of the first sick people. Zhou Zuofeng, who had no way of knowing he was presenting a danger to others, infected approximately 90 people, and they in turn infected others. Zhou Zuofeng luckily survived.

About a year after the outbreak, a member of staff at the Hotel Metropole took the elevator to the ninth floor. He carefully unscrewed the gold-colored sign with the number 911 on it from the door. Then he took another sign and screwed it onto the door where the old one had been. The room was now room 913. Because no one wanted to stay in room 911 anymore.

VIRUS PARADISE

You already know that viruses need living cells to survive. They jump from human to human via snot or spit or tiny droplets in our breath. They stick to elevator buttons and take up residence in carpeting, where they survive only briefly—if they were ever alive in the first place. They spread by hitching a ride with people. Without buses, trains, and especially airplanes, the SARS virus couldn't have hit us anything like as hard. Pandemics can only happen because there are so many people, and because people travel so much.

In the days of hunter-gatherers, there were also infectious diseases, but it was not easy for them to spread. A hundred thousand years ago, modern people—your ancestors—lived in nomadic groups in Africa. They later migrated to Europe and Asia, but the groups of people still remained at a considerable distance from each other.

So, there wasn't much for viruses to do. Once they'd infected all the members of a group, the virus party was pretty much over. The only viruses that hung on a bit longer were the ones that people didn't build up a resistance to.

Around 10,000 years ago, some hunter-gatherers discovered the benefits of the farming life. They were used to wandering around in search of fruit and other crops to pick, and animals to hunt. Someone must have thought: "What if we just put some seeds in the ground and harvest the grain? And how about putting a fence around those pigs and chickens instead of chopping them up for dinner right away?" And so, more and more plants and animals were found on their land. Which meant there were fewer reasons to travel in search of food.

10,000 YEARS AGO

100,000 YEARS AGO

People gradually became more successful at agriculture. More farms were created, followed by more villages and, later, towns and cities. There were as many people living in the whole world back then as living in the state of Michigan. But the population grew quickly because people stayed healthy for longer, and so they lived longer and had more children. There was time for activities other than just looking for food. Someone started making pottery, someone else invented the wheel, and others went on journeys of discovery to different parts of the world. And the viruses traveled with them.

There are now approximately 8 billion people on Earth. That's 500 times more than 10,000 years ago. They cut down forests to grow food. They build huge sheds and fill them with pigs and chickens. They buy their beef in Argentina, their flowers in the Netherlands, and their face masks in China. Most people live in cities, millions of them all together in one place. They swarm through malls and amusement parks. They sit packed into trains, sports stadiums, and movie theaters. Within one day, they fly from one side of the world all the way to the other.

Over the last couple of centuries in particular, our planet has become a paradise for viruses. If a virus infects just one person, it can conquer the whole world. Slowly at first, but then faster and faster. Read on to see what I mean...

NOW

FACTORY FARM

THE MULTIPLIER

With the help of social media, a funny dance or a grumpy cat can go all over the world in no time. You know: WhatsApp, TikTok, Instagram. "It's gone viral," we say, meaning that the video is spreading just like a virus. How quickly that happens depends on how infectious a virus is, or how many followers share a video. But even your little brother can do it, with just two faithful followers.

Suppose your little brother makes a funny video and his two followers watch it. Now imagine those two followers also have two followers, who have their own two followers, and so on. And what if each of those followers likes the video so much that they send it to their own two followers within twenty-four hours? The film would travel halfway around the world in little more than a month. Believe it or not, within thirty-two days, the video would reach 4,294,967,296 people. That's well over 4 billion!

Sadly for your little brother, that's not going to happen. Because most people won't share his video, no matter how funny it is. The same often happens with viruses. One person might be more easily infected than another. Or one person is much better at passing it on to others. There are all kinds of reasons for this, and researchers are still far from understanding all of them. It depends on the virus, too. Just as some of your little brother's videos are obviously funnier than others.

And yet his video could travel even faster than that. Because most people have more than two followers on TikTok or Instagram. Suppose his video is seen by someone with 100,000 followers. And what if that person shares it? Then suddenly there are a 100,000 people who get to watch the video. If only half of them share it, you've still reached 50,000 people in one go. That would take him half a month otherwise. The same thing happens with viruses. Some people are much more infectious than others. They're known as super-spreaders. If someone like that goes to a concert, they can infect lots and lots of people.

So, there are people who infect lots and lots of other people—and people who infect no one, or hardly anyone at all. On average, then, it's fair to say that everyone infects two other people. Then virologists say that the virus's "reproduction number" is 2, or the "R" is 2. This means that the virus spreads quickly, as you've seen from your little brother's video. If you want to keep a virus under control, you have to make sure that the reproduction number is under 1. At that point, within a group of people, one infected person will infect, on average, less than one other person. That means the number of infected people keeps going down, the R number gets smaller and smaller, and the virus slowly dies out.

But there's something that's not quite right about the example of your little brother's video. Something that means a virus can't simply go out and infect half the world. It's this: Some followers will have already seen the video when it was

posted by other people. So, they'll just ignore it and won't bother to share it. The more the video spreads, the more people have already seen it and just shrug their shoulders when it turns up again. You'll never get to 4 billion likes that way. And yes, it's exactly the same with viruses. Someone who has already been infected with a virus is less likely to become infected again and usually can't pass it on to someone else. They've built up resistance and are therefore immune. The more people who have had the virus, the more difficult it becomes for the virus to spread. In Chapters 3 and 5, you'll find out more about our brilliant immune system.

INVISIBLE CLOUDS

At a university in Tokyo, a darkroom has been set up with laser beams and a high-speed camera. The camera can make droplets of only 1,000 nanometers—a thousand times smaller than a millimeter—visible. Here's where the test subject comes in. He has an important task: he has to sneeze for the camera. That's easy enough with a bit of pepper sprayed up his nose: *aa-aa-aa-choo!*

With the naked eye, you can just about see the largest droplets. They fall to the floor almost immediately and don't travel far. But the camera also shows the thousands of tiny droplets that are invisible to the naked eye: microdroplets, or aerosols. These are so light that they travel much farther and can easily float around the room for up to fifteen minutes. They're also let loose when people cough, talk, laugh, or sing.

Imagine if your eyes worked the same way that high-speed camera does. Then you'd see that everyone in your classroom has a cloud of microdroplets around their head all the time. The biggest cloud would obviously be around the head of your teacher, who never stops talking. There would be smaller clouds around children who are secretly whispering to each other. And there'd be twenty or thirty rapidly growing clouds when you crack the best joke of the week. You'd also be able to see what happens when someone opens the windows. Within no time, the clouds disappear. Whenever someone opens their mouth again, new clouds form, but they quickly blow away.

Flu, colds, and coronavirus all spread mainly through big drops caused by sneezing and coughing. They soon fall to the ground. That's why many governments advised us to wear masks to trap the drops, and to keep a safe distance from other people. The virus can also be in microdroplets, but you have to ingest a lot of those droplets to get infected, so the risk is much smaller. But it's still a good idea to make sure that classrooms and other crowded spaces are well ventilated when the R number is high and lots of people are infectious.

Another trick is to make sure that the microdroplets become heavier so that they fall to the ground sooner. How? By keeping the air humid. That's particularly important in the winter. Hang wet towels over the radiator, get a humidifier or steamer, and bring in extra plants. That puts more water vapor in the air, which sticks to the microdroplets and makes them heavier. Instead of floating in the air, they go crashing to the ground.

There are some viruses that are even more infectious than the COVID virus, like measles and chickenpox. Those viruses do travel through the air, and not even a door will stop them. They go underneath or through the keyhole. Before a chickenpox vaccine was developed, 90 percent of children in the world caught chickenpox before they were twelve. Where vaccines are available, though, the number of cases has greatly dropped. Luckily, chickenpox doesn't usually have serious consequences for children, though it can be more dangerous when you're older. Measles is a bigger concern, and you've probably been vaccinated against it.

BE QUIET

So, not all viruses are equally infectious. It partly depends on how they move from person to person, and how long they can survive without a human being. You can pass on a simple cold or the flu without being anywhere near the other person. If you put your hand over your mouth when you sneeze and then walk downstairs and go through a door, the virus will now be on the handrail and the doorknob. The next person to go downstairs is likely to get the virus on their hand. If they touch their nose or bite their nails, they can become infected. That means it's best to sneeze into the inside of your elbow, not touch your face, and wash your hands thoroughly and often.

Viruses that travel through the air are difficult to stop. But there are also viruses that spread through all kinds of yuckiness, like puke and poop. Fortunately, those viruses don't spread so quickly. At least, I've never heard of puke and poop floating around in the air. There are viruses that spread through blood and sex as well, such as HIV, which causes the disease AIDS. You can learn how to protect yourself from such diseases. And then there are the viruses that spread via animals…

MAD ANIMALS

Evening is falling. Carrying your ball under your arm, you're heading home. What's that over there? There's an animal lying on the ground. Maybe a bird. At the edge of the path, by the bushes. Is it dead? Warily, you step closer. The animal is moving. It's not a bird. Is it a mole? No, it's furry like a mole, but a mole doesn't have wings like Batman. Batman! It's a bat! And it's sick or injured. Or it wouldn't be lying there. You want to help the poor bat, of course. You think about it for a moment. You're going to have to take the bat home with you, where you'll be able to feed it and take care of it. You put down your ball and slowly reach out toward the sad little pile of bat. Its mouth opens—and you see a row of sharp teeth, which isn't what you were expecting. You quickly pull your hand back. Very wise.

Bats can be infected with the rabies virus. Every year, 59,000 people around the world die of this virus. In Canada, the United States, and most of Europe, rabies infections in humans are now extremely rare, but when they occur it's almost always because of an encounter with a wild animal. Dogs, skunks, cats, monkeys, bats, and foxes, for example, can transmit rabies. So, it's important never to pet or touch a wild animal. Not even if a stray dog gives you a really cute look during your holidays in Mexico, or a monkey jumps onto your shoulder at a temple in Thailand. A bite, a scratch, or even a lick can transmit the rabies virus. Even in parts of the world where rabies hardly ever affects humans, bats might still carry the rabies virus, and cases can occur. It would be great if you could find someone to help you save the bat—because they really love to eat mosquitoes, for one thing— but you'd be wise to never pick a bat up with your bare hands.

Why is it a good thing that bats eat mosquitoes? Because mosquitoes are the most dangerous creatures on Earth! This is mainly because mosquitoes might carry a parasite that can give you malaria, a disease that causes more than half a million deaths worldwide every year, most of them, by far, in tropical regions of Africa. Malaria isn't caused by a virus, but some mosquitoes spread nasty viruses with scary names, like yellow fever, dengue fever, Zika, chikungunya, and the West Nile virus. Tiger mosquitoes, for example, live mainly in tropical regions, but they're expanding their habitat. Their eggs hitch a ride on bamboo plants that travel to Europe and North America on ships from southern China. In Italy and southern France, there's no getting rid of the tiger mosquito. As the climate is becoming warmer, they also like the idea of moving to more northern parts of the world, including the southern parts of Canada. But so far most tiger mosquitoes haven't succeeded in settling there. And people in northern climates want to keep it that way.

Mosquitoes don't transmit the virus deliberately. They need the blood of people and animals for their eggs. That's why you should always try to avoid getting bitten whenever you can—at home or on vacation—by using mosquito repellent, wearing long sleeves, and sleeping under a mosquito net. If a mosquito bites an animal that has a lot of the virus in its blood, the virus can enter the mosquito. Then the virus starts copying itself inside the mosquito. And if the mosquito then bites a person, she (male mosquitoes don't bite) can transmit the virus. Without ever meaning to.

But meanwhile, you're still stuck with that poor bat. How can you help it? Run home (don't forget your ball!). Call your city's animal control service, a nearby vet, or a wildlife sanctuary. They can catch the bat safely and take care of it.

TYPHOID MARY

Mary Mallon didn't mean any harm either. But wherever she went, typhoid fever soon broke out. Typhoid is a sickness transmitted not by a virus but by bacteria, so in a way she doesn't really belong in this book. But Mary Mallon is a great example of a super-spreader: someone who infects a lot more people than most others who have the virus—or, in this case, the bacteria.

Mary was a cook in the early 1900s who worked for one wealthy New York household after another. But it seemed that wherever she worked, typhoid fever would soon break out in the family. That was strange because typhoid was something that generally happened in poor neighborhoods, not rich ones. It was a nasty disease, too. Antibiotics hadn't been invented yet, and up to a quarter of the infected people in poor neighborhoods didn't survive. High time for an investigation!

The man who investigated the outbreaks soon realized that the cook, Mary Mallon, was the one thread that connected all the rich families who had been infected. But when he tracked Mary down, she showed no signs of being sick herself. Mary was definitely the source of the infection, but how? Well, the truth is that even a healthy person can infect others—and big time! In total, "Typhoid Mary" infected fifty-three people with typhoid, three of whom died.

Back then, not much was known about bacteria that spread diseases. So, it wasn't that unusual that Mary hardly ever washed her hands, even though she was cooking for the whole family. And cooked food can't spread the typhoid bacterium, because typhoid really hates heat. That meant there was only one recipe that could have been the source of all the problems: Mary's Sunday dessert, ice cream with fresh peaches. Mary had so many typhoid-fever

bacteria in her body that she often had them on her hands and transmitted them to the families she cooked for when she served her ice cream.

It's hard to say exactly what makes one person more infectious than another. And it's impossible to predict whether someone will infect a lot of other people or just a few. There didn't appear to be anything out of the ordinary about Mary Mallon, or about the super-spreaders in the SARS outbreak.

Do you remember Professor Liu Jianlun, who wanted to go to his nephew's wedding in Hong Kong? He infected at least fifteen other hotel guests, just by staying on the same hotel floor. Imagine what would have happened if he'd felt well enough to go to the wedding, with maybe

hundreds of other guests. That really would have been a super-spreading event, with even more infections than at the Hotel Metropole. And all those guests would have returned home the next day, to places all over China, and maybe other countries as well.

Super-spreading events happen where lots of people gather at the same time and in the same place as a super-spreader—for example, at a county fair, a soccer match, or a church service. As you can imagine, it makes a huge difference if you can prevent super-spreading events, because all those infected people can go on to infect other people. The virus uses their cells as copying machines, making millions of new virus particles. But how does it do that?

INTRUDERS

From superhero movies to dramas about criminal gangs, there are thousands of stories about the perfect robbery. You know— a gang wants to steal an expensive diamond, a famous painting, or a chest full of gold from a mansion, a museum, or a bank. Of course, the robbers do all the preparations for the, let's say, diamond theft. They go to the museum in broad daylight and look around as if they're ordinary visitors. *Aha, so that's where the guard stands. And there are the motion sensors. And there's the iris scanner that opens the door to the diamond gallery at night.* They spend months making a plan. The trickiest part is creating a copy of the museum director's eye—that's the only way to fool the iris scanner. The escape plan is important as well. Getting into the museum is one thing, but how do you get back out without the guards seeing you? Most crime movies are really tense—is the plan going to work?—but the plan nearly always succeeds. Unless there's a superhero around to stop them, of course. Sorry about the spoiler!

The way a virus particle gets into a cell is just as clever. Every virus has its own method, but the basic rules are pretty much the same. Let's take the coronavirus as an example. Usually, you get infected via your nose or your mouth, perhaps if an infected person starts coughing near you. Sometimes the virus particles go straight to your lungs. But that doesn't mean you're actually infected yet. An infection doesn't happen until a virus enters a cell.

With coronavirus, the virus particles have little spikes, a bit like a horse chestnut. They don't prick you because there's a tiny ball on the end of the spikes. That ball is the key to the cell. The cell's lock is called the ACE2 receptor, but you don't need to remember that name. It looks like a sort of feeler, and the ball on the coronavirus's spike fits it perfectly. When the key is in the lock, it can't come back out. The cell pulls the virus in, just as it sucks in useful substances. A kind of dimple appears in the wall of the cell. The virus sinks deeper and deeper, until the cell wall closes over it. That's the infection. You can imitate this by pushing an M&M into pudding: at first there's some resistance, but then the M&M sinks into the gloop until there's hardly any sign of it left.

When the infection has succeeded, the virus can get down to the real work. You already know that some viruses, just like people, have DNA that contains all their characteristics. Other viruses have a more primitive form of DNA, called RNA, but that's also a sort of code that describes exactly how to make the virus. The coronavirus is one of the viruses that has RNA instead of DNA. The virus releases its RNA as soon as it enters the cell.

The RNA has instructions like: "This is how to copy my RNA," and "This is how to make my skin," and "This is how to build my spikes," and "This is how to put it all together." The cell obediently follows all the instructions. And half a day later, the first new virus particles are ready. Thousands more will follow. Now all they need to do is escape from the cell. They do this in the opposite way from how the virus entered the cell. When they're near the cell wall, a small opening develops, which gets bigger and bigger and *floop*—there they go. Off on their way to new adventures. What will they do? Infect new cells? Or travel to the human's nose or throat so that they can hitch a ride on a sneeze or a cough and infect someone else?

3

WAR INSIDE YOUR BODY

You might not think so, but your body is heavily armed. Intruders like viruses will definitely meet resistance. With some viruses, though, the body needs extra help. The virus HIV, for example, slowly disarms your body before striking without mercy in the form of AIDS. Luckily, there are good medicines nowadays. But sadly, they came too late for the great singer Freddie Mercury, the lead vocalist of the rock band Queen. You can read about what happened in the Virus Story.

After that you can discover…
• why your snot is sometimes a funny color
• why fever is such a fabulous weapon
• about the undercover agents inside your body
• who goes to Intensive Care and who doesn't
• which viruses can save lives
• how it feels to lose your grandpa to a virus

In short: How viruses make you sick, and how you and your body react.

VIRUS STORY

ANTI-DEATH PILLS

AIDS is a disease caused by the virus HIV and spread via breastfeeding, sex without a condom, and used injection needles. AIDS was the biggest pandemic of the past century. Since 1981, more than 36 million people have died of this disease.

One of the most famous victims was Freddie Mercury, the singer of the rock band Queen. You know, the band that recorded "Bohemian Rhapsody," that song that always comes so high in the lists of most popular songs of all time. "*Galileo, Galileo, Galileo, Galileo, Galileo, Figaro...Magnificooooo,*" etc.—and you're still only halfway through the song.

Freddie Mercury didn't say that he was suffering from AIDS until one day before his death. But most people weren't surprised. When you're that famous, it's like being under a microscope all the time. Photographers from gossip magazines hid and waited for him in bushes, and journalists asked everyone who knew him if he was infected. Why did they think he might be? They knew Freddie was gay and, in those days, HIV was something that mainly affected gay men. When Queen stopped doing concerts in 1986 and Freddie started looking thinner and thinner, more and more people began to think he had AIDS.

AIDS is a disease that often doesn't strike until years after infection with the virus HIV. When people have just been infected, they feel like they've caught the flu, at most. They might have a fever, because their body's immune system is busily working away—that's the body's defense against intruders like viruses and bacteria. The fever is meant to destroy the virus, because many viruses don't cope well with higher temperatures. But that doesn't put off HIV. It goes on happily copying itself even when the infected person thinks the flu is long gone.

The nasty thing about HIV is that it attacks the most important cells of the immune system. It's as if your opponent in a soccer match first eliminates your goalkeeper and defenders so that their attackers are free to score as many goals as they want. There's no way you're going to win that game. And that's how it works with HIV.

The virus spends years demolishing the immune system. Meanwhile, the infected person often has no idea that they're infected, which means they can also infect other people. But there comes a point when the immune system is so badly damaged that it can't take much more. Other sicknesses, ones that aren't usually that serious, can hit hard now. The symptoms are more severe—high fever, extreme weight loss, exhaustion—and they just get worse.

A few singles by Queen came out in 1991. The video for "I'm Going Slightly Mad" was made in black and white, so that Freddie Mercury's unhealthy appearance would be less noticeable. But even a wig and a thick layer of makeup couldn't hide the fact that he was in bad shape. As for the title of the song, AIDS can affect a person's nervous system or mental health. Half a year later, another song came out: "The Show Must Go On." The video for that song was made using old clips from previous videos. The singer was too weak to record a new video. On November 24, 1991, six weeks after that song came out, Freddie Mercury died of AIDS, at the age of forty-five.

If he'd been infected at a later point, Freddie might not have died of AIDS. Since the virus was discovered in 1983, huge strides have been made in the treatment of the disease.

In 1985, a test came onto the market that allowed people to see if they'd been infected with HIV. But lots of people didn't want to find out, as an infection at that time meant that you would die no matter what. But if you didn't know you were infected, you had to be extra careful in your contact with other people. So, there was a growing focus on providing education and information, especially about safe sex.

Meanwhile, scientists all over the world were looking for medicines to cure or slow down AIDS. The pills that patients had to take caused lots of side effects and didn't do much good. In 1994, when the Dutch AIDS researcher Joep Lange suggested giving patients more pills instead of fewer, people said he was insane and threw tomatoes at him. And yet he was proved right. By using a combination of three different medicines—which people began to call the "HIV cocktail"—it was possible to slow the spread of HIV inside the body, enough

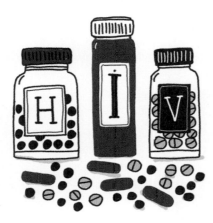

to keep the immune system working. Taking just one kind of pill didn't work, because there were always mutations of the virus that the pill couldn't handle. This treatment was expensive and tough to handle in the beginning. People had to take up to thirty pills a day—and the side effects were no fun.

Now that treatment was possible, however, a lot more people took the HIV test. If you were infected, you had to take these drugs for the rest of your life. But that life would be almost as long as it would have been without the HIV infection. Also, since 2007, the three drugs have been combined in one pill, which you have to take only once a day. AIDS went from being an inevitably fatal disease to a disease that could be treated. Well, if you could afford it.

Treatment with HIV drugs is still expensive. That's partly because they're patented. That means the manufacturers of the drugs are the only ones who are allowed to make them. So, they can also set the price. Luckily, patents don't last forever, and more and more drugs are now also affordable for poorer countries. However, there are still big differences throughout the world. In total, 38 million people worldwide are infected with HIV, and 25 million of those people live in Africa, the vast majority of them in the south and east of the continent.

In spite of the use of these drugs, more than 600,000 people worldwide still die of AIDS every year, over half of them in Africa. This isn't only because medicines are too expensive for many Africans. There are other reasons that are at least as important. Many of the issues arise from differences in culture. People who grow up in a culture where no one talks about sex are going to have a hard time learning to protect themselves from sexually transmitted infections. And there are still many places in the world where LGBTQ+ people are labeled criminals, so how are they going to learn about HIV transmission and safer sex practices?

In Tanzania, men can even end up in prison for life for having sex with another man. Gay relationships are forbidden there. Which is why you won't find any information in the Freddie Mercury Museum about his love life. Because that museum is in the house where he was born, on the island of Zanzibar, which is part of Tanzania.

RESPECT FOR THE RUNNY NOSE

The average person sneezes at a speed of 40 miles (65 kilometers) per hour. But some sneeze droplets have been measured at a speed of roughly 90 miles (150 kilometers) per hour. That would get them a big fine for speeding on the freeway. But what is the point of all that sneezing? Well, your body thinks you need it to clear your airways. "No!" the viruses and bacteria cheer. "It's so we can spread even more! Yay!" Well, they're both right.

Sneezing, coughing, sore throats, and runny noses are all symptoms of a cold. And colds are caused by...a virus. Actually, there are something like two hundred viruses that can cause colds. So, it's possible to catch a cold a few times in a row. Normally when your body gets rid of

a virus it remembers how it did that, which means the virus doesn't stand a chance the next time. It's a complicated story, and I'll spare you the details for now. But because there are so many viruses that cause colds, the next cold virus that comes along may strike just as hard.

It's super annoying, of course, all that sniffing and coughing. But remember that those symptoms are signs that your body is dealing with the virus. By coughing and sneezing, your body is trying to eject the virus particles. The sore throat happens because extra blood and moisture flows to the inflamed place, flooding it with antibodies

UH-OH

HELP! I'M DROWNING!

and immune cells. This makes it swell up, and that's painful. Your snot is packed with antibodies against intruders. That's why it starts streaming when you have a cold, and why it turns white or green. Those colors are a sign that lots of extra immune cells are working to combat the intruders. So, maybe you should show a bit more respect for the tickle in your throat and your stuffed up nose.

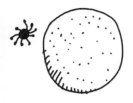 

Symptoms don't just come from your immune system. The virus particles that are copying themselves also have an impact. When they're done with a hijacked cell, they usually leave it dead. That causes more and more damage in your body. And that results in inflammation, which might give you a sore throat, earache, or stomachache. With coronavirus, that inflammation can really get out of hand. All kinds of organs are damaged. The alveoli—those are the air sacs in the lungs— become inflamed. They swell up, so there's less and less room for air. That makes it hard for patients to breathe and, in the worst cases, they have to be put on an artificial breathing machine, called a respirator.

With a lot of diseases, you can tell from your symptoms that there's something wrong inside your body, and that you might be infectious. But some viruses are so sneaky that they don't cause any symptoms at all, or they wait for a very long time before causing symptoms. Just look at HIV. Freddie Mercury became infected but didn't develop severe symptoms until years later. He could have passed on the virus to other people in the meantime, without knowing it.

The Ebola virus is a lot more honest. The symptoms happen before you're infectious. And those symptoms are pretty clear, as you'll see. This helps against infection in two ways. People with symptoms stay home because they're so sick. And the symptoms are a warning, so that others can stay out of the patient's way or wear protective clothing. Which is handy. If you hit a ball wrong, it's best to warn other people right away: "Hey, look out!"

With viruses like HIV and coronavirus, it works the opposite way. You're already infectious before you have symptoms. It's as if the ball has already hit someone's head and that's when you shout, "Look out!" Usually, the symptoms begin a week or so after the coronavirus infection. This week is called the "incubation period" of the virus. So, you get infected, happily go walking around for another week—and then finally realize you're sick. Luckily, our bodies are full of virus fighters, which nearly always help us to get back on our feet pretty soon. How they do that is the complicated story that I can't hold off telling you any longer.

VIRUS FIGHTERS: PART 1

Lots of viruses are tiny little troublemakers. That should be clear to you by now. But your body nearly always outsmarts them. The vast majority of virus particles never manage to get anything done at all. They get stuck in your snot, are gobbled up by an immune cell, or get neutralized by antibodies. That's all the work of your body's defense force, known as your immune system. And the fact that you're still alive is the proof that you have one.

Your immune system is made up of billions of cells, with thousands of different functions. There are guards, spies, messengers, and fighters, all with their own superpowers. They can be found in all your organs and tissues and they have a sophisticated system for communicating with one another. That is much needed, because your immune system has three different departments: a set of physical barriers, your innate immune system, and your adaptive immune system.

The physical barriers are obviously what you know best. They include your skin and your mucous membranes, which is the skin on the inside of your mouth, nose, and so on, where it's usually a bit, um . . . slimy. Your skin is virtually impenetrable—unless you get a cut. Your immune system quickly goes into action when you scrape your knees. In no time at all, the wound is sealed up with a scab. But there are openings in your body that the enemy could just march straight into. Your mouth, your nose, your ears—they're like the gates of a castle. That's why they're so well guarded by saliva, snot, and earwax. Most viruses and bacteria that try to enter via these gates get stuck, like heavily armored knights trying to cross a swamp.

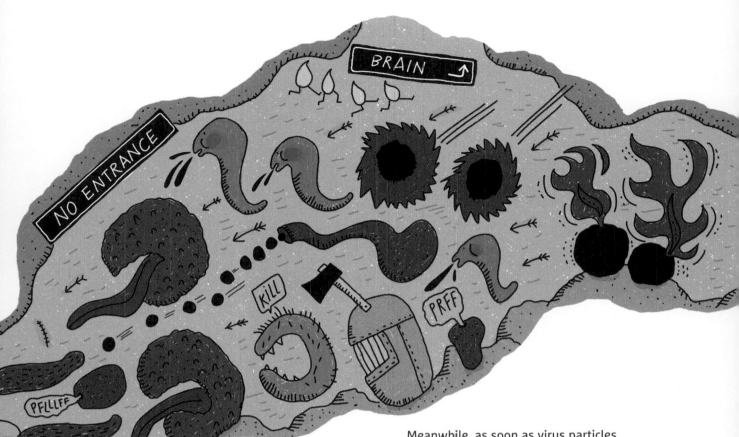

That slimy gunk is where you'll also find the warriors of the innate immune system. There are immune cells hanging around there, constantly checking if any strangers are trying to get in. Peanut butter sandwich? Okay. Unknown virus? Get lost! As soon as an intruder manages to make it through one of those gates, all kinds of immune cells go into action. The antibodies do whatever they can to block the virus. The immune cells all have different roles, from fighter to errand boy. Scientists have given them way more complicated names, such as macrophage, lymphocyte, and neutrophil. I personally prefer the natural killer cell, though. The name makes it very clear what that particular kind of cell does to intruders: it kills them off, one by one. What a hero!

Meanwhile, as soon as virus particles penetrate your body's cells somewhere, various substances are released and are on their way to your brain. Inside your brain is where the dial for your body temperature is located, and the substances are the signal to give that dial a big old turn. It's a brilliant idea, because fever is an amazing tool for dealing with unwanted intruders. You know that viruses try out all kinds of mutations in their search for new victims. So, viruses that are out to get people are completely adapted to the conditions inside the human body, just as arctic hares are adapted to life in the cold and dromedaries are adapted to life in the desert. Viruses work best at a temperature of 98.6 degrees Fahrenheit (37 degrees Celsius), because that's the average temperature of you and me. If it's two or three degrees warmer, viruses don't like it anymore. They replicate themselves up to two hundred times more slowly. And at that temperature, our immune system actually works much better. That'll teach the virus!

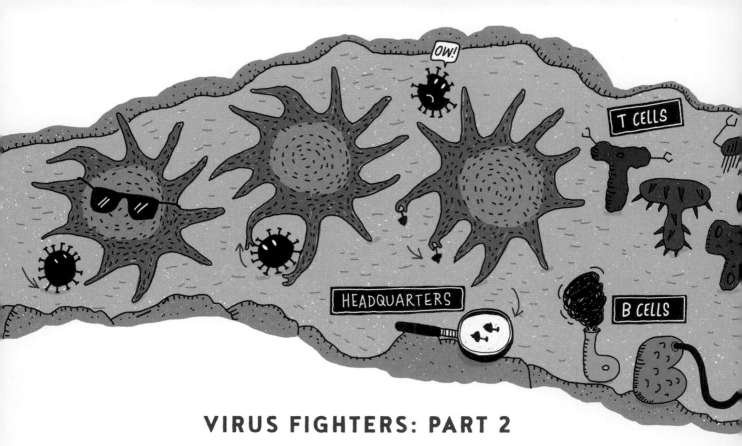

VIRUS FIGHTERS: PART 2

Previously in *Snot, Sneezes, and Super-Spreaders*: in spite of the brave resistance from snot and saliva, a virus has managed to get inside. Natural killers and other immune cells are keeping the intruder occupied. To gain time, the temperature inside the body has gone up. A rapid response is needed from virus fighters who know exactly how to deal with this virus.

Your innate immune system is a sort of basic defense system that you already had when you were born and which remains the same all your life. The advantage is that it's always ready and can immediately react to danger. But it always does this in the same way. Whether it's flu, COVID, HIV, or measles: this immune system defends itself with the same weapons. It's as if you defended a castle with a bow and arrows every time, even if a new enemy suddenly appeared at the gates with completely different weapons. You're obviously going to grab

your bow and arrows because you don't have anything better. But if the enemy arrives with rocket launchers, you'd better come up with a different response.

That's why we have our adaptive immune system, which is a system that learns. This process involves selecting new weapons that are perfect for combating a specific virus. It all takes a bit longer than the reaction from the innate immune system, but the good thing is that it never forgets the weapons it used. So, if the same virus turns up at the gates again, your body doesn't have to go looking for the right cells and antibodies. It can instantly respond with custom-made weapons. This means that most viruses don't stand a chance the second time around. That's when we say that you're immune to the virus.

The contact between these two systems is made by the dendritic cells. Like undercover agents,

B cell is just a little bit different from the others, like an endless bunch of keys, only one of which will fit the lock. And the piece of virus that the dendritic cell has smuggled in is the lock that all the keys need to be tested in. This requires as much patience as guessing a number between one and a billion. But luckily your immune system works a lot faster than your brain.

If cells are found that work on this virus, everything goes up a gear. The T cells start multiplying like crazy. This creates an entire army of T cells that's sent straight to the front line to help the immune cells in their battle. As they're made specially for this purpose, they can also deal with the virus particles that the other immune cells have trouble with.

they try to identify the enemy's weapons. When they're tracking one down, they grab the virus particles, break off bits of them, and take them to the headquarters of the adaptive immune system. They do this via the lymphatic system, a special network in your body that transports substances that are important for your defenses. The headquarters are located in the "nodes" of the lymphatic system. The best-known lymph nodes are your tonsils, but there are also nodes in your armpits, neck, and stomach. When they're working hard, they swell up and you can even feel them.

As soon as the cells turn up with their evidence, the whole headquarters speeds into action. Billions of immune cells are waiting there. They're divided into T cells, which can help to fight the virus, and B cells, which make antibodies. Hopefully, somewhere among those immune cells, the answer to this specific virus can be found. Every T cell and

The B cells turn into little factories, continuously producing antibodies that the virus doesn't know how to handle. The antibodies stick to the virus particles like superglue. The result: the virus particles clump together, and they can no longer enter any cells. The glue also acts as a signal to the immune cells: "Come over here and clean up!"

Your immune system can easily beat most viruses. Including our new coronavirus. But older people in particular can have real problems with coronavirus. They usually notice this when they become short of breath. That's when the immune system can't handle the virus, or has to fight just a bit too hard. More and more fluid enters the lungs and, if you're unlucky, the lungs also fill up with dead cells and virus particles. Sometimes a few cowardly bacteria also take advantage of the situation and cause pneumonia. When that happens, it's time to go to the hospital.

IN THE HOSPITAL

Disinfect your hands. Put on your gown and do it up tight. Wear your mask and check it's on right. Wear your protective goggles. Pull on the latex gloves and make sure they cover the ends of your sleeves. Now you're ready to come take a look at the hospital. Or that's how it works during a pandemic. When there's no major infectious disease around, there isn't quite as much protective gear. Although, of course, you never know if a feverish, coughing patient is about to walk in with an unknown illness—as they discov-ered at the hospital around the corner from the Hotel Metropole in Hong Kong.

Coronavirus patients usually arrive at the hospital's Emergency Department. That's also where you go when, say, you've cut off your fingertip in woodworking class or had a serious fall from your skateboard. In the Emergency Department, the doctor assesses how the patient is doing. She has equipment to measure the most important bodily functions, such as blood pressure, temperature, and oxygen levels in the blood. And she obviously asks the patient what their symptoms are. In the case of coronavirus, the most urgent symptom is usually difficulty breathing.

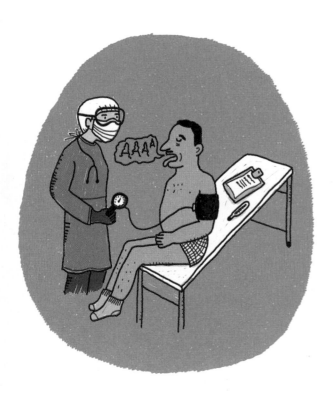

RECEPTION ↰
WAITING ROOM ←
EMERGENCY ←
COVID UNIT →
INTENSIVE CARE ↑
SWEAT *IT OUT AT HOME* ↴

Based on this examination, the doctor decides what to do with the patient. That process is called *triage*, a French word that means "sorting." Some patients are sent straight to Intensive Care, some are sent home to recover, and others are admitted to the COVID unit. In the COVID unit, they're often given extra oxygen through a tube in the nose or a mask over the mouth. They may also be put on an IV drip, a bag of liquid that drips into your body through a needle. This extra support is usually enough to allow the body to recover. Within a few days, the immune system has beaten the virus, and the patient can go home.

But sometimes the disease gets worse. If that happens, the patient is moved to Intensive Care. Nurses monitor the patient day and night. There's all kind of equipment around the bed to help them. COVID patients who end up in Intensive Care are usually put into a coma. A tube is inserted deep into their throats to send air to the lungs. This artificial breathing is necessary until the immune system has defeated the virus. That can take weeks, and it's really tough, particularly for older patients, or those who have other significant health challenges. So, sometimes a patient will talk to the doctor and decide that the best thing to do is to stay in the COVID unit, take painkillers to help get some rest, and hope that the lungs clear up and everything gets better.

In spring 2020, hospitals became far too busy with all the COVID patients. In some hospitals, even in wealthy countries like Italy and the United States, patients had to lie in the corridors because there was a shortage of space. When that happens, triage becomes a very tricky task. What do you do if you have only one free bed in Intensive Care, but ten seriously ill patients are admitted? Should the youngest patient have the bed? The oldest? The sickest? The healthiest? The richest? The one who has an important job? No one wants to have to make choices like that. That's one of the reasons why we did everything we could to limit the number of infections, and that's how hospitals were just about able to handle the number of sick people in most countries. But it was a close call. Ambulances had to transport patients to other hospitals, sometimes even to hospitals in other countries. Operations on other patients were postponed. Doctors and nurses worked long days and nights in their hot protective gear, saw all kinds of horrible things, and often became sick themselves. With so many virus particles hanging around, medical staff had a heightened risk of becoming infected, even in protective clothing. And at that time there was no effective medicine yet.

MUMMY AS MEDICINE

Pharmacy shelves are full of pills, potions, ointments, drops, and bandages. But they don't have a drug that will cure a cold or the flu. It is possible to put the brakes on viruses—remember those drugs to treat HIV infection—but curing viral diseases is very difficult.

Pharmaceutical companies do everything they can to develop new medicines. There are two good reasons for that: they can make people better, and they can make a lot of money. Imagine if they came up with a pill to cure the most dangerous viruses. Everyone would want to have it, and they could sell the pills for a super high price. Particularly if the drug was patented, meaning the company was the only one allowed to sell it. This can make drugs unaffordable, particularly for people in poor countries.

The drugs that helped fight HIV were patented, but the government of South Africa didn't care. Millions of South Africans were infected with HIV, so the government told local companies that they were allowed to make the same drugs and sell them for much less. Forty big pharmaceutical firms filed a lawsuit against the government in 2001 because they owned the patent. But there was so much protest that they gave up. Which is only right—why should only rich HIV patients be allowed to stay alive? It's too bad, though, that Mantombazana Tshabalala-Msimang became the South African minister of health. She claimed that drugs to treat HIV were toxic and said people were better off eating beetroot, lemon, garlic, and

MANTOMBAZANA
TSHABALALA-MSIMANG

potatoes. This advice likely contributed to the deaths of countless HIV patients.

During any outbreak, epidemic, or pandemic there are always people who come along with "miracle drugs." In the past, it was hardly surprising that people were willing to try anything available. They didn't know about viruses and bacteria so they had no idea what might make them better. If you see people dying of the Plague or a deadly flu, then you're only too happy to try out toad's blood or herbal tea or powdered mummy to see if they happen to work. Sometimes just thinking that something works can help you, too. That's called the placebo effect. You probably used to fall for this trick yourself when you were little. Someone gave you a Band-Aid or a kiss on a sore spot—and it actually helped.

Nowadays, medicines have to meet strict requirements in most countries. They must be clearly effective against the sickness, and they can't come with too many side effects. That's why manufacturers carry out extensive trials, with half of the test subjects given the real drug and the other half a fake medicine, a placebo. None of the test subjects or researchers are allowed to know who's been given the real drug. Later, they gather the evidence to see which of the patients in the trial have improved. Of course,

you would expect the real medicine to be much more effective than the placebo. If the patients who were given the real drug get healthier, without troublesome side effects, then that shows that the drug is effective, and the manufacturer can seek permission to start selling it.

Scientists also carry out research into the use of viruses as medicine. Viruses that make people healthy—that's a change! But it's exactly what the bacteriophage can do. Remember? That's the virus that looks like a lunar lander, which specializes in destroying bacteria and doesn't mind if you just call it phage. There's a good chance we'll be able to use it to replace antibiotics in the future.

Antibiotics are a fantastic recipe against diseases caused by bacteria. The word originally comes from the Greek words *anti* meaning "against"

and *bio* meaning "life." So, antibiotics work well against living creatures, like bacteria, but not against viruses. If you have a bacterial infection, the doctor sometimes gives you a prescription for an antibiotic. And that's great, because the antibiotic will kill a lot of the dangerous bacteria in your body. The bad news is that it will also kill the good ones, like the bacteria that help your gut digest food, so you might need some time to recover from it. Another disadvantage is that more and more kinds of bacteria are getting used to antibiotics and becoming resistant to them. That's making them harder to fight.

This is where the phage comes in. The advantage of the phage is that it kills only the harmful bacteria. The disadvantage is that you first have to know what the harmful bacteria are, so that you can send exactly the right kind of phages after them. So, we'll have to see if these healing viruses actually end up in pharmacies.

I feel way better

Without side effects?

FAREWELL THROUGH A WINDOW

Sadly, sometimes the body loses to the virus. By the end of 2021, more than 5 million people worldwide had died of COVID. In the United States, that number was 774,000. In Canada, it was 30,000. And in the Netherlands, where I live, it was over 20,000. One of those people was the grandfather of ten-year-old Jesper, thirteen-year-old Veronique, and fourteen-year-old Ulrieke, from the village of Huisseling in the Netherlands. Grandpa Ard was sixty-four.

Ulrieke: It was at the start of the coronavirus crisis. There wasn't a real lockdown or anything yet, but we already knew about the virus and that you had to be careful. So, we didn't visit Grandpa and Grandma. We only saw them during video calls. They were really, really careful. They didn't go anywhere, and they didn't actually have any visitors either. So, we have no idea how he caught it.

Jesper: Grandpa was in the police choir, but that had stopped for a while, so it can't have been that.

Veronique: When we heard that Grandpa wasn't feeling good, I hoped it was just the flu and not COVID. That was on Saturday. A week before he died. On Monday he had a high fever, 102 degrees (39 degrees Celsius) or something like that, and he was getting more and more tired. By Thursday, he was finding it hard to breathe, and he was so weak that he didn't come downstairs. They called the doctor, who took him straight to the hospital with Grandma. He was put in isolation and examined and tested, and they found out that night that he had COVID. He had asthma, too, which lowers your chances of survival. So, he wasn't allowed to go to Intensive Care. Because there were other people with a better chance.

Jesper: It was tough that we couldn't visit him. But we still had video calls with him. He was on a breathing machine, with a mask over his mouth. The three of us sat together at the kitchen table. We didn't really know what to say at first, but Grandpa was still making jokes. We saw them giving him an ice cream and we said, "We want one too!" And we showed him the fireworks. People were setting off fireworks here in the distance and we turned the webcam to show him, and then it was just a nice chat.

Veronique: You could see that he was sad we couldn't be there, too.

Ulrieke: Because they already knew even then that he didn't have much chance of surviving. We were going to have a video call with him again on Saturday, but Grandma sent a message that it wasn't going well. In the afternoon, I was doing my homework and Mom came in, with tears on her face. She said Grandpa had died. That was really weird. I couldn't actually believe it. It had happened so quickly.

Veronique: Grandma had been with Grandpa the whole time. So, she had to go into quarantine, and we couldn't give her a hug to comfort her or anything. We could only see her through a window. We had to keep our distance from her at the funeral as well. We went to see Grandpa first. His casket was in their garden shed, and you were allowed to take turns to go in. But it was all behind glass, because they were afraid he might still be infectious. Then we drove to the crematorium, and we lined up and said goodbye to Grandpa.

4

VIRUS STOPPERS

Viruses are annoying, but measures to stop the spread
of viruses aren't exactly a barrel of laughs either. Okay,
schools closed down, and that seemed like fun for a while.
But when your dad started trying to explain long division,
I'll bet you couldn't wait for your school to open up again.

It might be comforting to know that people have struggled
with infectious diseases for centuries. That's why this Virus
Story is about one of the deadliest pandemics in history.

After that you can discover...
• how a virus experiences a lockdown
• when it's time to rescue your fish
• why penguins were waddling down the street
• how science saves lives
• how useful a sniffer dog can be during a pandemic
• how a village went into quarantine for
  fourteen months

In short: How to frustrate a virus.

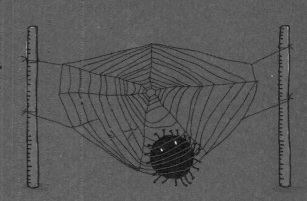

A PRISON SENTENCE FOR A SNEEZE

The sun is shining. The streets are quiet. Schools, museums, and movie theaters are closed. Most people are inside, with the windows open, and their hands raw from washing them all the time. The few people who are out on the streets are wearing masks. When they see someone they know, they greet each other a little awkwardly, without shaking hands or hugging. They keep their distance as they have a chat. Does that sound familiar? Welcome to 1918, the year of the deadliest flu in history.

Just be happy that you live more than a century later, in a time with proper health care, in a country where there's no famine and most people are healthy and have strong immune systems. In 1918, that wasn't the case in a lot of places. As a result, within two years, a highly contagious flu virus was able to kill between 50 and 100 million people. That was around 3 percent of the world's population at the time. So, that means if you lived in a city of 100,000 inhabitants, an average of 3,000 people died of the virus. Nearly every child lost a mother, a father, or a teacher to what was then known as the "Spanish flu" (today, it's more commonly called the 1918 flu).

The name makes no sense, by the way. There are all kinds of ideas about where the Spanish flu began, but Spain isn't one of the candidates. Spain was the first country to mention the disease in a newspaper, though. Lots of other countries had soldiers fighting in the First World War, and people didn't want to hear more bad news. It would have made the spirits of the soldiers and the citizens sink even lower. But Spain wasn't participating in the war. So, the first accounts of a nasty flu that could kill people within just a few days appeared in the newspapers there. The news reached other countries via the Spanish newspapers, and so it came to have the name "Spanish flu." It could just as easily have been the French, Chinese, or American flu. The best-known story about where the flu actually originated starts in rural Kansas, right in the middle of the United States.

A hundred years ago, rural Kansas was a poor area, where farming families lived close together, often in one room with their chickens and pigs. In January 1918, a local doctor began to worry about the large number of sick people in the region. Usually, the flu is over within a few days, and it doesn't kill healthy young people. But this time it was different. The symptoms were more severe, and even healthy young farmers died of it. Luckily, not too many people lived in the area, and within two months the epidemic was over. The local people mourned the victims and went on with their lives.

Just 280 miles (450 kilometers) away was a military camp, Camp Funston. You could hear the sound of bullets, grenades exploding, and sergeants yelling as they trained tens of thousands of young men to become soldiers. When they were done training, these new recruits would take the train to the harbor, where the steamships to Europe were waiting. They were going to help the French and the British, who had been fighting a tough battle against Germany, Austria, Turkey, and other countries for years: the First World War.

The men slept close together at Camp Funston, in barracks with 250 beds. They came from all over, including rural Kansas. So, it wasn't too surprising when, on March 4, an army cook reported to the camp hospital with fever, a headache, and a sore throat. That same day, hundreds of other soldiers developed the same complaints. Within no time, the hangars at the army base were being used as hospitals and they were full of coughing, groaning, and sweating patients.

But the mobilization continued. The help from America was desperately needed in Europe. Thousands of soldiers from Camp Funston were put on the train to the east coast, even if they had flu symptoms. Soldiers from all kinds of different camps came together at the ports. Squeezed in together, the men boarded the steamships. They were afraid of the horrors of war and had no idea that their worst enemy was invisible and was traveling with them.

A week later, the soldiers went ashore in France. If the virus had had legs, it would have been jumping up and down with happiness. An entire new landmass lay at its feet, populated with hundreds of millions of Europeans and Asians, many of them hungry and weak after years of war. They lived close together in small, stuffy houses, and worked in packed mines and factories with no ventilation. And best of all: the soldiers that the virus traveled with were mingling with their French and British counterparts. Sleeping alongside one another in large barracks. Watching the enemy from narrow trenches, long, damp channels in the ground where it was hard to remove the sick and the dead.

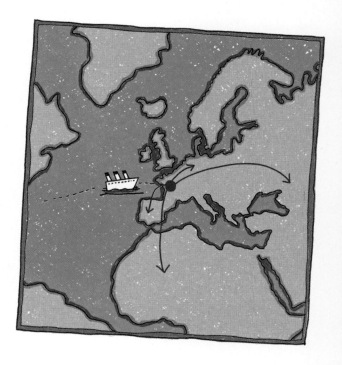

As a result, the 1918 flu spread rapidly through-out France. By May 1918, there were victims in Great Britain, Italy, Spain, and North Africa. Germany was spared for the time being, but as soon as they captured prisoners of war, they caught the virus, too. That allowed this strain of flu to strike in Germany, Poland, and Russia. There were even reports of infections in India, China, and Japan. The virus moved so swiftly that it soon became weaker. Anyone who survived the virus wasn't likely to become reinfected. And anyone who didn't survive could no longer spread the virus. So, by the beginning of the summer, the 1918 flu seemed to be dying out. But not for good.

That was just the first wave. And, all in all, it wasn't too bad, even though it caused tens of thousands of deaths and made many more people sick. Inside all those bodies, the virus was free to copy itself to its heart's content. Billions of copies of the virus were made, some more successful than others. One of those copies was a lot more deadly and infectious than the original. That mutation had a slightly different exterior, and the immune systems of people who had already had this flu didn't recognize it. And so the nightmare began all over again, but worse this time.

At the end of the summer, the second wave swept across the globe. In many places, schools, churches, and movie theaters closed. Meetings with lots of people were moved outside or can-celed. People were advised not to shake hands. They were told to wash their hands thoroughly, and to open windows. In some places, people had to wear masks. Most people didn't object, but there were some groups that resisted. They felt that the government couldn't force them

to wear masks, and that masks did more harm than good. In the United States and Australia, you could receive a hefty fine or a prison sentence for not wearing a mask. If you coughed or sneezed on the street without covering your mouth, you risked a prison sentence for that, too. The court cases took place in the open air.

In spite of all those measures, there were tens of millions of deaths. The virus hit hard, particularly in poor areas, where people lived close together and were hungry and already in poor health. That meant they had little resistance to the virus. The same was true of the soldiers in Europe, who were still fighting a war. Roughly a third of the soldiers who died in the war were victims of the 1918 flu strain. If you include civilian deaths, the 1918 flu killed far more people in one year than the war did in four years. Between 50 and 100 million people were killed by the virus—and around 20 million by enemy weapons.

Luckily, on November 11, 1918, the armistice was signed, ending the war. The virus was happy to hear that news, too. Hundreds of thousands of soldiers returned home, where they were welcomed with open arms. The whole world was celebrating. And the virus was chuckling away. Or it would have been if it had a mouth to chuckle with.

ANY QUESTIONS FOR THE VIRUS?

Masks, lockdowns, keeping your distance… People weren't happy about those rules in the past, and they're not happy about them during the coronavirus crisis, either. They see mandatory face masks as an attack on their freedom. They're angry about the impact of the lockdown on their ability to earn a living. And if they have to keep their distance from other people, they miss their grandma's kisses. It's all very annoying, of course. But what do viruses think about these measures? We asked a virus that's been through two lockdowns…

"I think I speak for all virus particles when I say that those kinds of measures don't make life easier for us. At first, when no one knew what was going on, we were free to do our own thing without anyone bothering us. People were packed in together on the subway, at concerts, and standing in line for the roller coaster. Back then, you didn't need someone to sneeze for you to make the jump. Even if you were inside one lonely person, you could still reach another body. People sneezed into their hands and spent just a couple seconds washing them, sometimes even without soap. Which we obviously thought was hilarious. From the fingertips, it's an easy hop to a keyboard or a doorknob, and then all you have to do is wait for someone else to pick you up. If they rub their eyes or pick their nose, then you're in—and the copying can begin all over again. But… what was your question? Oh yes, whether we're bothered by the measures. Yup, I should say so.

"Look, ultimately we all need a body so that we have a nice place where we can copy ourselves. And when we're done, our copies need to go in search of other bodies. So, you come out with a sigh or a snot bubble, hoping to find a new body. But at some point—it was March, I think, it was so tragic—all those newborn virus particles were ready to make the jump, but there were hardly any human beings around. Everyone was staying home. It was really boring. No one was going to parties. No one was hopping onto the train or going to the movies with their friends. They were all playing games, doing jigsaw puzzles, or working on projects at home in their rooms. That meant the end of billions of virus particles. They were coughed or sneezed out and . . . that was it. So sad. They would never be able to enter a cell and copy themselves. Sometimes you could jump to your body's housemate, but that was it—you didn't get any farther than that. And often they went and deliberately spent time alone when they were infected. Which was a dirty trick. That made it harder and harder for us to spread, and so there were fewer and fewer of us.

"Luckily, people decided that they'd had enough, and they started going back outside, to school, to shops . . . They thought they were rid of us, and they started to get careless. And so we could make the jump more often again. At first it was the young people. They really wanted to party, and they didn't usually get so sick. But they were infectious, for their parents and for their teachers, too. And some-times we made the parents sick. And they went to visit *their* parents. And *they* got even sicker. So sick that they had to go to the hospital. That was when people finally began to realize that we never really went away. So we sat with them on the sofa and watched all the government people on TV an-nouncing all kinds of rules again. Which was a bummer for us. Anti-virus measures are no fun for human beings—and they're certainly no fun for viruses."

THE PROBLEM WITH LILIES

The virus is right about one thing: anti-virus measures are no fun for human beings. Wearing a mask is one thing, but when people aren't allowed to travel, to shop, and to go out as much, companies make less money, and they have to let employees go. Millions of people worldwide have lost their jobs and are a lot poorer. So, it makes sense that governments aren't exactly keen to announce lockdowns. But if you wait too long, the virus has free rein, and even tougher measures are needed. It's a terrible dilemma, one that you can see for yourself...

Imagine you have a big garden pond with a water lily that doubles in size every day. If that continues, the pond will be completely covered within thirty days, and all the fish in the water will suffocate. For the first few days, the lily can hardly be seen. By day 20, it's covering only one thousandth of the pond. That's 0.1 percent. It's no big deal, you think. And indeed, on day 25, 97 percent of the pond is still uncovered. You can see the fish happily swimming around. You think to yourself: *When the lily's covering half of my pond, I'll do something about it.* But actually, when you stop to think about it, you should realize that you have only one day to save the fish. And getting rid of the lily now is twice as much work as it would have been yesterday, four times as much work as the day before yesterday, and more than a thousand times as much work as ten days ago. If you don't believe me, do the math.

10

More or less the same thing happened with the coronavirus. No one intervened when it was still small, and when it became clear how big it was, drastic measures were needed to get it under control. There's also the fact that the coronavirus is always undercover when it starts its attack. It's already contagious even when you have no symptoms. So, it's a while before people get tested. Some of them get sick. Then they usually stay home in bed. With some people, the sickness doesn't get worse until a week later. Then they go to the hospital and, if it gets even worse, to the Intensive Care Unit. In many countries, the alarm bells only start ringing when the hospitals become too busy. They're afraid they won't be able to treat the patients, so the number of infections has to come down. The government consults experts and chooses the measures that make the most sense. Wear your mask! Stay home! Close the shops!

Then you just have to hope that things will quiet down at the hospitals. But you won't know that for two or three weeks. Because that's how long it takes for someone who's infected to end up seeking medical attention. And in the meantime, people are shouting: "More measures! Do more!" Of course they are, because there are still more sick people, who were previously infected, being added to the numbers.

At the same time, other people are shouting: "Fewer measures! Do less!" Of course, they want their freedom back, and to be able to earn money as usual. And then there are people who say all the measures are unnecessary. Because, they say, in terms of the number of people affected, the coronavirus is only a little worse than a bad flu. And maybe that's true for the situation

with anti-virus measures in place. But we have no way of knowing what things would be like *without* those measures—because we've never tried. Studies have calculated that, without the anti-virus measures, COVID would have caused at least twenty times as many deaths, with all the associated misery: mass graves, mass mourning, and so many sick people that, for example, doctors, the fire service, and garbage collectors would have been unable to do their jobs.

Looking back, you might say: I should have dealt with that water lily sooner. Then it would have been much easier. Or: We should have locked down our country before the virus got here.

But most people wouldn't have put up with that, because they didn't see any threat yet. There would not have been widespread public support. Just as there's no support among most children for wearing bike helmets. It's only when they bang their heads that they think: *I wish I'd worn a helmet.*

ON THE OBSTACLE COURSE

Be honest: had you ever heard of a lockdown before 2020? Had you ever worn a face mask, waved at your teacher via your webcam, or washed every little crease of your hands? Well, I certainly hadn't, in any case. My teacher didn't even have a webcam. But because of that stupid virus, everyone's gotten to know all about anti-virus measures. They don't make you invulnerable, but the more you follow them, the less chance there is that you'll get infected, and the harder it is for the virus to spread. So, with anti-virus measures, you're making a sort of obstacle course for viruses. But how do those obstacles actually work?

Distance

The lockdown is an extreme form of keeping your distance, so that the virus can't get to you. If you're around other people, you need to watch out for surprise sneezes. That's why the advice is: keep your distance, so that the average sneeze can't reach you. Strangely, the distance is bigger in some countries than others. In France, it's 3 feet (1 meter) apart; in Canada and the United States, the recommendation is 6 feet (about 1.8 meters); in Australia and the Netherlands, it's about 5 feet (1.5 meters); and in Sweden it's 6.5 feet (2 meters). So... are the French the weakest sneezers?

Lockdown

Suddenly there were penguins on the sidewalk, goats on the highway, and wolves trotting politely over the crosswalk. The streets of many cities were so empty that wild animals came by to take a look. The idea of a lockdown is simple: make sure people stay home as much as possible, so that they meet fewer people and can't infect one another. That's why people have to work from home, why shops and schools shut, and why, for example, sports competitions are no longer allowed to take place. If we do all that, there's not much fun to be had for viruses.

Fresh air

The longer you spend together in one room, the more aerosols enter the air. You remember—aerosols are those little droplets that you can see only with a high-speed camera. Particularly if you talk a lot, sing, or play your trumpet, the number of aerosols around you will quickly rise. If someone's infected, that could include aerosols with virus particles. That's why you have to keep your distance inside, too, and it's good to open two windows, so that the air flows freely and is refreshed constantly. Are you cold? Put on a coat, or air the place thoroughly during a break.

Soap

You know from ads on TV that dishwashing soap makes greasy pans clean. That's because soap mixed with water dissolves fat. That's good—because the exterior of viruses is actually a layer of fat. Washing your hands with soap and hot water destroys viruses. You have to make sure you rub soap into all the nooks and crannies of your hands for at least twenty seconds, though. When you rinse your hands, the virus particles disappear down the drain in tiny little pieces.
Byeee!

Don't touch!

Suddenly you weren't allowed to touch anything, not your face, not your grandma, or the light switch, or the handrail, or the shopping basket...maybe nasty little virus particles were lurking in all those places, waiting to infect you. That chance is very small, but it's better not to take the risk. Besides, it works in two ways: if you don't touch the light switch, you can't get a virus from it, but you also can't leave a virus on it, which could infect other people. But if you simply wash your hands well, before and after touching something, then that's pretty...handy.

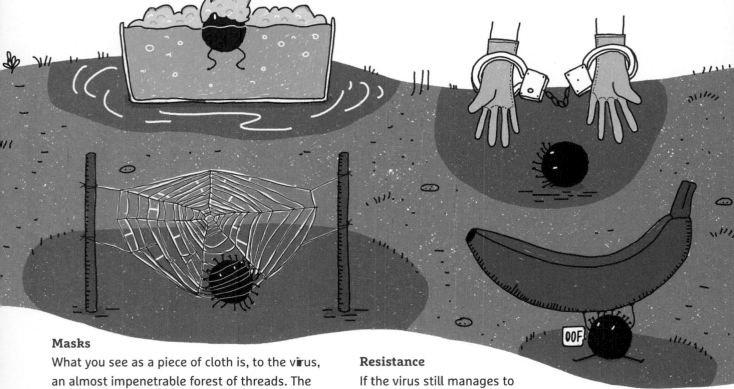

Masks

What you see as a piece of cloth is, to the virus, an almost impenetrable forest of threads. The aerosols containing the virus particles try to float through, but as soon as they hit a thread, they get stuck. However, with poor-quality masks, there are always a few droplets that make it through. That's why it's important for everyone to wear a mask properly. The chance of virus particles getting through two forests is really small.

Resistance

If the virus still manages to reach you, a good immune system can help a lot. A healthy diet, exercising regularly, sleeping well, and not being stressed all help to create a strong immune system. That won't necessarily help you to avoid infection with the virus, but it will help your body to fight against the disease. Healthy people recover more quickly.

SCIENCE VERSUS DIARRHEA

In times of pandemic, people claim all kinds of things. That beetroot helps to beat AIDS, for example, and that herbal tea is effective against COVID. But to find out what really works, you first have to do research. In the nineteenth century, cholera hit Europe. Cholera is a sickness that almost literally drains people. It's a kind of death by diarrhea. In those days, most scientists thought you got cholera from the bad air around marshes and big cities. But the English doctor John Snow didn't believe that at all.

Snow noticed that cholera occurred not only in cities and near marshes, but also in places with clean air. The patients he spoke to told him that the disease began with stomachache. That's not what you'd expect from something you breathe in. It sounded more like it might be caused by something you eat or drink. So, Snow suspected that people were infecting one another through water. A suspicion of this kind that has not yet been proved is called a hypothesis. Next, Snow had to do research to confirm his hypothesis.

This was the beginning of epidemiology, the study of how diseases spread. If you know how a disease spreads, you also know how to prevent infections, which means you can save lives.

In early 1854, Snow investigated where people in London got their water from. In the wealthier neighborhoods, the water came from companies that took it from the River Thames. Some of them did this upstream, where the water was still pretty clean. Others did it downstream of a sewage pipe that discharged stinking brown gunk into the river. Snow knocked on thousands of doors. He asked if he could have some water from the tap, and if there had been any deaths from cholera in the house. He could tell from the salt content of the water which company it had come from. When he compared that to the deaths, he found a lead: thirty-eight of the forty-four dead people got their water from the company downstream of the sewage pipe.

JOHN SNOW

BROAD STREET

CHOLERA PATIENT ●

Other scientists weren't convinced. They insisted that cholera was caused by dirty air. Later that year, there was another outbreak, and Snow continued his research. In the district of Soho, houses had no running water, and residents fetched their water from nearby pumps. Snow went around the houses again to ask about deaths. At many, no one answered the door because the people were already dead or had fled town. So, he asked the local authorities for the details. He recorded the deaths in the area on a map, and he marked where the water pumps were. What did he see? The outbreak was clearly situated around the pump on Broad Street. Oddly, though, people who didn't live near the deadly pump or a neighborhood with a cholera outbreak still caught cholera. Snow wanted to find out how that had happened. It turned out that three victims were children who drank from the Broad Street pump on their way to school, and others were people who did the same on their way to work.

John Snow had enough evidence for his theory. Even the priest and researcher Henry Whitehead, one of the biggest supporters of the dirty-air theory, was convinced. On September 8, 1854, the local authorities removed the handle from the Broad Street pump to prevent any further infections. But how had the water become contaminated in the first place? Snow and Whitehead searched for the first

case of cholera in the area. It was a baby whose family lived not far from the pump. The baby had fallen ill with diarrhea, and the mother had emptied the baby's diapers into a cesspool, a pit where the contents of people's toilets ended up. This one was close to the pump. It turned out that this cesspool did indeed leak into the water that fed the Broad Street pump. That was how the cholera was able to contaminate the water. But what with, exactly?

In the same year Snow carried out his research, the Italian Filippo Pacini discovered the cholera bacterium, but his discovery received little attention. Thirty years later, the famous German microbiologist Robert Koch received all the credit when he, too, made cholera visible. And once they could see it, they could find where it lived: mostly in water or in food contaminated by poop.

John Snow was just happy to have proved his theory. His work is a textbook example of the scientific method. On the basis of observations (cholera also occurs in places with clean air), he came up with a hypothesis (cholera is spread by water). He carried out research (interviews, a study of the existing literature, chemical analysis of water), made connections (on the map), and drew conclusions, which his fellow scientists (Whitehead and others) were free to challenge. So, the next time someone recommends a miracle cure, like beetroot or herbal tea, just ask them for the scientific proof.

PACINI

CHOLERA BACTERIA

KOCH

TEST, TEST, TEST

Cholera bacteria came to England on a boat, and SARS caught a plane to Toronto. Bacteria and viruses do not respect borders. That's why, in 1851, France organized a meeting of twelve countries to discuss the best way to tackle cholera and other epidemics. This group expanded and was the forerunner of the World Health Organization (WHO), which was founded in 1948. Almost all countries are now members of the WHO. Roughly 8,000 people work for the organization, and their goal is to make everyone in the world as healthy as possible. They do this by carrying out research, giving advice, and fighting diseases.

The countries that belong to the WHO have an agreement that they will report dangerous infectious diseases immediately. Your own doctor knows all about this, too. If you go see her and you have all the symptoms of smallpox, then she'll call the local medical authorities immediately, and they'll contact the WHO. Although it would be kind of strange if you had smallpox, because that disease was eradicated in 1979—thanks to the work of the WHO. The important thing is to make sure infectious diseases are detected as soon as possible, so that we're able to contain them. With SARS, it was stopped just in time. But COVID got out of hand within a few months. Some people say that's because China reported the disease too late, but the undercover infections and the increase in air traffic meant there was probably no way of stopping it anyway.

TEDROS ADHANOM GHEBREYESUS

Once a disease is widespread, it still makes sense to map out all the cases, as John Snow did with the pump on Broad Street. Which is why there has been such a huge focus on testing during the COVID crisis. "Test, test, test!" said the boss of the WHO, Tedros Adhanom Ghebreyesus, from Ethiopia. And so, many millions of cotton swabs have been stuck into throats and up noses and temperature guns have been pointed at foreheads. Recently, even dogs have learned to help: research suggests that dogs can be trained to sniff airport passengers and detect coronavirus infection. They certainly are man's best friend!

SNIFF

Other pandemics were no different. In the Middle Ages, doctors drew black crosses on the doors of people they'd diagnosed with the Plague. Ships carrying crew members with infectious diseases had to raise a yellow or red flag, so no one would come on board. At the time of the 1918 flu pandemic, cases of smallpox and cholera had to be reported, but not the flu, and by the time doctors started keeping track of all infections, it was far too late.

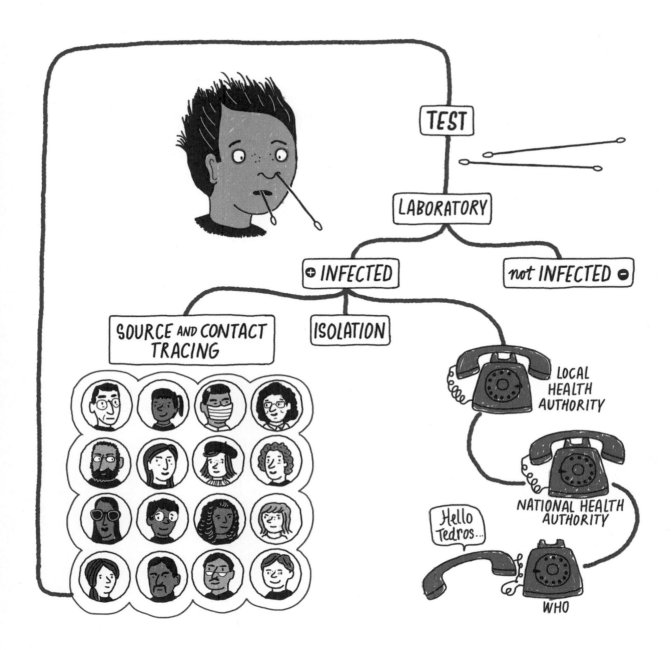

It's important to know who is infected. That way you can make sure they don't infect other people, and you can also investigate who they've been in contact with. In 2014, that worked well during an outbreak of Ebola in the West African countries of Liberia, Sierra Leone, and Guinea. Ebola is a rare viral disease that kills about half of those who are infected. Contamination happens through just about all the fluids that come out of your body:

pee, poop, vomit, blood, sweat...So, doctors and nurses have to wear thick, sealed suits to treat patients. The doctors in Liberia asked as many patients as possible who they had been in contact with. That allowed them to warn and isolate people who might be infected. Ensuring those people had no contact with anyone else meant the virus was unable to spread any farther.

QUARANTINE, THEN AND NOW

Whether this actually happened is not entirely certain, but the idea is as disgusting as it is brilliant. In 1346, the Turkish army commander Jani Beg wanted to reclaim the city of Kaffa from the Italians. For two years, thousands of his soldiers besieged the city walls with shields, swords, and bows. The men died in masses, many killed by the enemy's arrows, but even more by the Black Death, also known as the bubonic plague, or simply "the Plague." Before long, all those corpses smelled so bad that it gave Jani Beg an idea. He had them loaded onto catapults and fired over the city walls. For hours, Plague-infected corpses rained down on Kaffa. The plan exceeded all expectations. The corpses infected the enemy and contaminated the drinking water. As soon as the Italians realized a terrible disease was spreading, they fled back to Italy. And the Black Death sailed with them.

In the five years that followed, at least 75 million people worldwide died of the Black Death. The cause of this disease was not a virus, but bacteria in the fleas that live on rodents. Flea bites transmitted the Black Death to humans, who then become infectious via their breath and their stinking wounds. Soon, anyone who was diagnosed with the disease had to stay inside so they couldn't infect anyone else. Later, many cities had special Plague houses outside the city walls. All the victims were kept there in quarantine. They weren't allowed back out until they'd recovered. Or died.

The word "quarantine" dates from this time. It comes from the Venetian word for forty, because ships had to wait forty days before they were allowed into the harbor. That was how long it took to see if any crew members were developing symptoms. If they didn't, the ship could finally dock.

The outbreak of the Black Death in the fourteenth century was the deadliest outbreak of the bubonic plague, but certainly not the last. In 1665, there was a new outbreak of the disease, this time in London. Towns and cities in the surrounding area closed their gates to keep out the disease, but in September a tailor in the village of Eyam received a bundle of cloth from the capital. As with cholera, people believed that the Plague was caused by dirty air, or that it was a punishment from God. So, fleas in a parcel of cloth didn't appear to be a reason for concern. And yet, the village was doomed. The tailor's assistant was just the first of hundreds of victims of bubonic plague in the small village.

When the inhabitants realized how infectious the disease was, they made a brave decision. They shut themselves off from the outside world to prevent the Plague spreading to nearby towns and villages. For fourteen months, they were alone with their fellow villagers and the Plague fleas. Local farmers left food for them at the village boundary, so that they didn't starve. Entire families died of the Plague, but the villagers' self-imposed quarantine saved countless lives because the disease didn't reach big cities like Manchester and Sheffield. That's something to think about if you ever have to go into lockdown again. It could always be worse.

Nine months after the coronavirus outbreak, people in China were going to parties and amusement parks again, and everyone could happily hug one another. But in other parts of the world, hospitals were full, restaurants were closed, and people were facing travel restrictions and wondering whether they'd see their families over the holidays. Why was that? In China and some other Asian countries, the pandemic rules were very strict from the beginning. If you get infected in China, you go straight into quarantine. And it's taken seriously. You're not allowed to leave your room for fourteen days. They use GPS to keep an eye on you. Meals are left outside your door. Every day you're contacted by telephone, or you have to use an app to check in. Meanwhile someone is investigating all your recent contacts, using camera images, bank statements, and serious questioning. All those people also go into quarantine and are tested. This means the virus has no opportunity to spread anymore. Which is just as well, because a thorough approach like this is impossible if you have an overwhelming number of infections.

5

A FASCINATION WITH VACCINATION!

Whoa, those lockdowns and face masks—what a hassle!
Not to mention the fear of getting sick. Luckily, we have
vaccines: the best prescription against deadly viruses.
They save millions of lives every year. There's no superhero
who can compete with that. In fact, one virus has completely
disappeared from the face of the earth. Well, almost completely...
You can read about it in the Virus Story.

After that you can discover...
• how milkmaids helped science
• why vaccines make you a bit sick
• how you can help to protect babies
• what to do if you want to become an ex-doctor
• what aluminum yells as it enters your body
• how rabbits helped to fight mad dogs
• how to go through the looking-glass and get all the
  way to the land of snot, sneezes, and super-spreaders

In short: How vaccines protect us.

TAMING THE VIRUS

In the twentieth century alone, smallpox caused hundreds of millions of deaths. But it has since been tamed. Smallpox now exists in only two places in the world: in around 120 bottles in a heavily guarded lab in Yekaterinburg in Russia, and in 450 bottles in a heavily guarded lab in Atlanta in the United States. The room where these bottles are kept is completely isolated from the rest of the building. There are no cracks, no holes, and you can only enter via a special secure doorway. Only people with special training and a kind of airtight spacesuit are allowed in. The lab has negative air pressure: the air pressure is lower in there than it is outside. That way, no air can escape. Which means no virus can escape if a bottle ever breaks. But there's not much chance of that happening.

The bottles are kept inside a stainless-steel cylinder in a freezer at -320 degrees Fahrenheit (-196 degrees Celsius). The freezer is attached with thick chains to steel bolts in the floor or the wall. We don't know exactly how, though, because the lab doesn't want bad guys to have any more information. There are rumors that the freezer is in a room that's disguised as a broom closet, and that there's a fake freezer with a sign saying, "Last bottles of smallpox virus in the world," but they might well contain apple juice. By the time the bad guys figure out they got it wrong, the alarm will have gone off and the security guards will be dealing with them. It would be an absolute disaster if the virus ever escaped from the lab, whether by accident or stolen by terrorists or a wicked dictator.

In 1967, the World Health Organization began a campaign to wipe out smallpox worldwide. Wherever smallpox was found, people were given a vaccine. That made it impossible for smallpox to spread. Ten years later, the Somali cook Ali Maow Maalin was the last person to become infected with naturally occurring smallpox. When everyone he had been in contact with had received the vaccine, the world was free from smallpox. Many people consider this the greatest achievement of medical science. Within a dozen years, the world's deadliest infectious disease had been completely wiped out. Except for those few bottles. It's a good thing they're so closely guarded.

ALI MAOW MAALIN

As the disease has been gone for so long, most people now alive have never been in contact with it. That means they haven't built up immunity. If you look at America's history, you can see what that means.

In the fifteenth century, only the original inhabitants of America lived there. People like the Aztecs and the Incas created entire civilizations with impressive temples, legal systems, and extensive armies. To ward off disaster, they sacrificed thousands of children, guinea pigs, and llamas, high up in the mountains. But that couldn't prevent the disaster that was heading their way.

CHRISTOPHER COLUMBUS

In 1492, a Spanish ship under the command of Christopher Columbus landed on the coast of the island of San Salvador, in what is now the Bahamas. As soon as the Spanish king heard that Columbus had "discovered" a new continent, with all its potential riches, he sent more ships carrying 1,200 men. This was hardly alarming to the Aztecs, who had more than 100,000 soldiers themselves. But, though no one knew it, the Spanish soldiers were carrying secret biological weapons: cholera, yellow fever, malaria, measles, the Plague, and smallpox.

Before 1521, on the spot where Mexico City is now, the Aztecs had their own capital city: Tenochtitlán. At that time, with 200,000 inhabitants, Tenochtitlán was one of the biggest cities in the world, with magnificent temples, gardens, and fountains. In 1519, the Spanish army, led by Hernán Cortés, was warmly welcomed by the Aztec leader Moctezuma. But the many treasures that Cortés saw made him greedy—

MOCTEZUMA   HERNÁN CORTÉS

and he seized power. So, the Aztecs rebelled and drove him out. The Spaniards didn't stand a chance.

Soon, though, the secret weapons began to work. Aztec after Aztec suffered from high fevers and blisters all over their skin. Smallpox had got them. Soon the dead were piling up. At least 30 percent of the Aztecs died of the disease, including Cuitláhuac, Moctezuma's successor. In 1521, Cortés returned to besiege the city. The population was so weakened that the last Aztec leader, Cuauhtémoc, gave up after three months. That was the end of the Aztec Empire. But Cortés still found it necessary to raze the magnificent city of Tenochtitlán to the ground.

After Cortés's victory, two of his men struck out, headed in different directions. Hernando de Soto had it easy during his march through North America. Smallpox had traveled ahead of him, and he found wiped-out cities everywhere. Francisco Pizarro, with fewer than two hundred men, traveled south and attacked the Incas in Peru. The Inca Empire had millions of

inhabitants and tens of thousands of soldiers, but it was also weakened by smallpox and other infectious diseases. The Spanish had other advantages: their horses and swords. In 1572, the last leader of the Incas, Túpac Amaru, was beheaded on a square in the city of Cuzco. A hundred years later, only 1 million of the original 6 million Incas were left. In that short period of time, the Aztec population had gone from 20 million to under 2 million.

But why were the Incas and Aztecs hit so much harder by smallpox than the Europeans were? It was because these people had not been exposed to the disease and so had never had the chance to build up immunity. In Europe and Asia, for thousands of years, people had lived together with cows, pigs, sheep, goats, and a lot of other farm animals that carried viruses and bacteria. These viruses and bacteria had plenty of opportunity to make an easy jump to humans. So, at first, many people died, but over time, more and more people developed immunity—an immunity that the Incas and Aztecs didn't have.

They had their own diseases in Central and South America, of course, ones to which the Spaniards had no immunity, but relatively few. The only farm animals they had in that part of the world were llamas, alpacas, and guinea pigs. But they didn't produce much milk, and they certainly didn't lay eggs. They were mainly good for meat, wool, and for transportation (well, not the guinea pigs). So, people came into

much less contact with animals, and there were fewer diseases as a result. Which was great. Until the Spaniards came along.

So, now you see why Spanish is spoken in much of Central and South America, and why those last few bits of smallpox are so closely guarded. Without immunity, we're defenseless against smallpox. Luckily, we have emergency plans and vaccines in place in case smallpox suddenly returns somehow. But wouldn't it be better to destroy those last few bits of virus as well? Heated discussions regularly arise about this subject. Some people say that those last few bottles are a danger to humankind. But others are afraid that the smallpox virus might pop up again somewhere, and we might need to have some virus on hand to make a vaccine.

THE FIRST VACCINE

It's August 9, 1721. In London, a group of prisoners who have been given the death sentence are offered a choice between the gallows and taking part in a scientific experiment. That choice is easily made. Under the watchful eyes of twenty-five scientists, the six "volunteers" are given incisions in their arms and legs. Very carefully, the doctors rub a little pus from the blisters of a smallpox patient into the wounds. The prisoners now know for certain that they won't die by hanging. But are they going to die of smallpox?

Within a few days, they start to show symptoms, but then all six of them recover. One of the prisoners is made to sleep in the same bed as a young smallpox patient for weeks, and yet she does not become infected. King George I pardons the prisoners: they are free to go. Six months later, the king has his daughters inoculated against smallpox. The lesson? Exposing people to a tiny bit of smallpox protects them for the rest of their lives.

In Asia, Africa, and rural Europe, people had known this for a long time. They used to infect healthy people by using a straw to blow powdered smallpox scabs up people's noses, or by rubbing some smallpox pus into a wound, as happened with the London prisoners. This taught the immune system to recognize the virus so that it would make antibodies and T cells to protect the body next time the virus came around.

However, this old method is dangerous. It works with the active virus, which remains infectious to others during the treatment. About 2 percent of the people who received this treatment died. They took the risk only because a natural smallpox infection kills even more people, and at the time hardly anyone escaped the virus. Fortunately, the English doctor Edward Jenner found a safer way to create immunity.

In 1796, Jenner carried out a medical experiment, one that would get him sent to prison these days. Back then, it was well known that, for some reason, milkmaids never suffered from deadly smallpox. When Sarah Nelmes, a milkmaid, came to see him with a cowpox rash on her hands, Jenner had a bright idea. Cowpox is highly

BLOSSOM

SARAH NELMES

HMM...

EDWARD JENNER

EXPERIMENT 1

COWPOX

EXPERIMENT 2

EEK

SMALLPOX

contagious, but nowhere near as dangerous as smallpox. Jenner thought that milkmaids might have immunity from smallpox because they were frequently exposed to cowpox. To test his hypothesis, he looked for a young and healthy person to experiment on. He found the perfect person in his gardener's eight-year-old son, James Phipps.

Jenner took a little cowpox pus from Sarah and rubbed it into a cut on James's arm. The boy had a few mild symptoms and then recovered. But the dangerous part of the experiment came six weeks later. Jenner made another cut in James's arm and infected him with the fresh virus from an actual smallpox patient. If Jenner's hypothesis was right, the boy would have no problems. But if he'd gotten it wrong, James might die. For days, James and his parents lived in a state of hope and fear. But he didn't get smallpox. And he didn't get it when Jenner brought him into contact with the virus again, either. Jenner repeated his experiment with other people, with the same result every time. His hypothesis was proven.

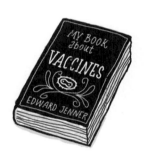

MY BOOK about VACCINES
EDWARD JENNER

Vaccine against SMALL-POX

Two years later, Edward Jenner published his findings in a book. He called his method "vaccination" and the drug a "vaccine," after the Latin word for cow: *vacca*. Most of Jenner's colleagues were enthusiastic, but there was also some opposition. Some people believed that diseases like smallpox were a punishment from God, and that it was wrong to defy the Lord's will. Others warned that a cow's head would sprout from your body after inoculation with the smallpox vaccine. But if that were true, the streets nowadays would be a pretty funny sight—because nearly everyone who's over the age of fifty received the smallpox vaccine as a baby. As a result, there's no longer any need to be afraid of this deadly disease.

YES!

GETTING SICK TO STAY HEALTHY

"An ounce of prevention is worth a pound of cure." That's one of those old-fashioned expressions that you might expect to hear from your grandma. But grandma's right. If you make sure you don't get sick, you don't have to go to the hospital. And if lots and lots of people make sure they don't get sick, a whole country doesn't have to go into lockdown. And then I wouldn't have had to write the two previous chapters.

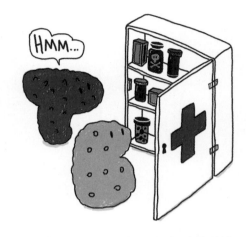

Vaccines really are a great way to prevent disease. Together with soap, antibiotics, and sanitation, they've ensured that people all over the world stay healthier for longer and live to be much older. In 1900, people worldwide lived to an average age of thirty-one. (In Europe, the average was forty-five, in the United States it was forty-eight, in Canada it was fifty, and in Australia it was fifty-one.) In 2017, the worldwide average was seventy-two. The eradication of smallpox alone has given millions in the world a much better chance at a long life.

Vaccines work by getting your adaptive immune system, the learning one, to go into action. If you're good at learning as well, you'll remember what that is: the part of your immune system that looks for exactly the right weapons to deal with intruders. But to do that, it has to know who the

intruder is. That's why it takes a while before the weapons are ready, but it's worth the wait. Your body usually remembers which antibodies and T cells go with which intruder. So, the virus doesn't stand a chance next time around. You're immune. The only downside is the time it takes to look for the right weapons. In that time, a virus can sometimes hit hard.

Vaccines tell your immune system in advance which weapons it will need when a particular intruder comes by. As a result, you're already immune before you're infected. The trick is to find a vaccine with the same characteristics as the virus, but less dangerous—a sort of pretend virus that allows the immune system to practice safely.

Jenner's vaccine worked because cowpox is related to smallpox. The cowpox virus has the same spikes, and that allows the immune system to learn which weapons will be needed when the real virus comes along.

But you can teach your immune system a lesson in other ways, too: for example, by using dead or broken bits of a virus. They're no longer able to multiply, and they can't make you sick, either. But because they have exactly the same spikes as the active virus, your immune system knows which weapons it needs. And it gets them ready for the next time that particular virus comes by.

A new method, which was used for the first time in some coronavirus vaccines, makes use of pieces of synthetic RNA. This RNA tells your cells to make spikes, just like the virus. When your immune system notices the spiky cells, it makes the antibodies and T cells that are needed. Job done. The spikes and the RNA disappear by themselves.

Vaccines make you a little bit sick, so that you won't be really sick later. Usually, you don't notice it at all, but some vaccines do have side effects. You might get aching muscles, a headache, or a slight fever after the shot. You can tell from the side effects that your immune system is learning. And that's exactly the point.

A SHOT FOR EVERYONE

Baby Micha was eight months old when he caught the measles. He was still too young to have been vaccinated against this disease. Micha had a high fever, kept vomiting, and ended up in Intensive Care with double pneumonia and inflammation of the heart. For a week, he fought for his life. Luckily, he made a complete recovery. He'd had the disease, so he was now immune to the measles, but he still received the anti-measles vaccine because it comes in one shot with the vaccine for mumps and rubella. He got that shot when he was fourteen months old.

● MUMPS
● MEASLES
● RUBELLA

There's a good chance that you received this shot—the MMR vaccine—as well. And probably other vaccines, too. In most countries, the government recommends a schedule for the vaccines you should receive. Depending on where you live, you might have received different vaccinations in a different order, but basically the first diseases we protect infants against are diphtheria, pertussis (whooping cough), tetanus, polio, and hepatitis B. A bit later, you got your vaccine against measles, mumps, and rubella. These are the diseases that are particularly dangerous for the very young.

Polio, for example, used to be known as infantile paralysis. About 1 percent of the children who catch it are no longer able to use certain muscles, and this usually results in a deformity of an arm or leg. In 1988, the World Health Organization started a program to wipe out polio worldwide. Thanks to the vaccinations, the number of polio cases globally has fallen from 350,000 a year to only a few hundred.

Ask your parents if you can take a look at your vaccination record. It says exactly which shots you've already had. If you've ever traveled to a far-off country, it might include a few more uncommon vaccinations. That's because there are different diseases in different countries—like rabies, for example, which has been virtually eradicated in many parts of the world but is still common in others.

Some vaccinations are for young and old, like the ones against coronavirus and the flu. Depending on where you live, you might need to get certain vaccinations in order to do certain things. For example, in some parts of Canada you need to have a set of vaccinations to attend school. All fifty American states require some kind of vaccination for school, but which diseases you need to be vaccinated against will vary. Australia and the United Kingdom don't make school vaccination mandatory, but strongly encourage it.

Nobody will force you to get a vaccine—you or your parents will decide, taking into consideration the risks and benefits. It's your body and your life. And, by the way, the choice you make about vaccination will affect the lives of others, too. Maybe I should explain.

All vaccines are not equally effective. Some are 95 percent effective at preventing illness, while others might reduce the risk of getting sick by only 10 to 20 percent. Also, some people can't receive certain vaccines because of allergies. And children under the age of twelve months can't be protected against measles yet—remember baby Micha? For the sake of those people, it's important that as many people as possible are vaccinated, so they can't pass on the virus.

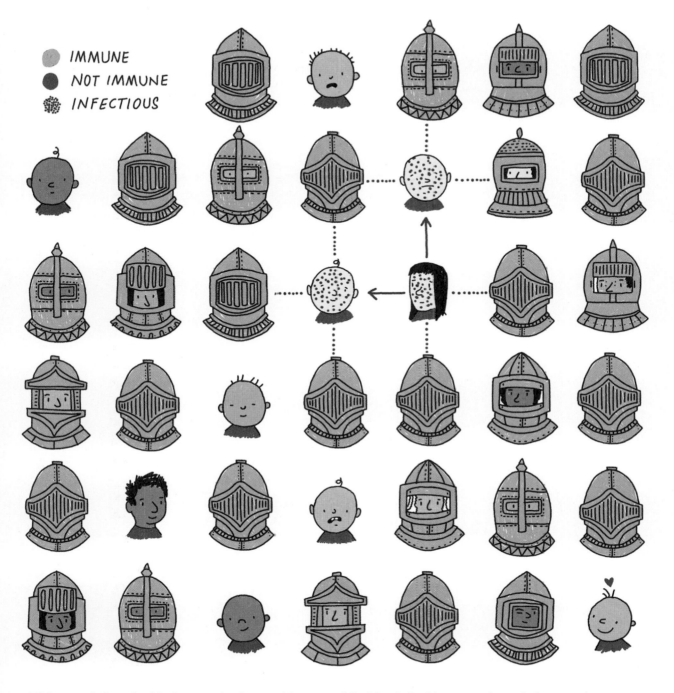

IMMUNE
NOT IMMUNE
INFECTIOUS

Micha was infected with the measles by an older girl who came to the after-school daycare center. She was old enough to have had the vaccination, but her parents didn't want her to be vaccinated. That decision almost cost Micha his life. If the girl had been vaccinated, or maybe if all the girl's friends had been vaccinated, the measles would never have reached Micha. That's how herd immunity works: the more people in a group who have become immune to a disease, through infection or vaccination, the safer it is for the group as a whole.

DANGEROUS NONSENSE

Samoa is made up of two beautiful islands in the Pacific Ocean, but at the end of 2019, life there didn't feel much like paradise anymore. A year earlier, two babies had died after receiving the MMR vaccine. Anti-vaccine groups seized the opportunity to shout at everyone who would listen: "You see? Vaccines are dangerous!" Within a short time, the number of vaccinated babies fell to 31 percent. Parents were wary of allowing their children to receive a vaccine that had killed two babies. But…the children hadn't died because of the vaccine. They'd died because the nurses had made a mistake and accidentally mixed the vaccine powder with an expired muscle relaxant anesthetic instead of water.

That mistake had far-reaching consequences. When a traveler who was infected with measles landed in Samoa in August 2019, the virus quickly took hold. Almost 6,000 Samoans in a population of 200,000 caught the measles, and there were more than 80 deaths, mostly of young children. Every family with an unvaccinated child had to stay inside and hang a red cloth on the door. Everyone hoped that the vaccination team would come knocking before the virus did, because you can bet the parents wanted their children to have vaccinations now. In Samoa, 95 percent of the population is now vaccinated against MMR. That should be enough to make the measles disappear from Samoa altogether.

What we saw in Samoa can be seen in other places, too. Opponents of vaccinations—known as "anti-vaxxers"—are using the internet to reach more and more people. You obviously know that not everything on the internet is true. Try searching for "UFO" or "flat Earth"—you'll see all kinds of nonsense. But it's still pretty spectacular nonsense. YouTube and Facebook make good

use of this. They want visitors to their sites to stick around for as long as possible, so they dish up more and more spectacular items. It's also what you get if you search for "vaccine" + "autism." What you read and see then is all the fault of one man: Andrew Wakefield, a British doctor who hasn't been allowed to call himself a doctor since 2010.

Autism is a condition that can make it difficult, for example, for someone to have contact with and communicate with others. In 1998, Andrew Wakefield did some research into the connection between autism and the MMR vaccine. According to Wakefield, the vaccine could cause autism, so it would be a good idea to stop using it until more was known about it. Some newspapers and broadcasts thought this was spectacular news and pounced on it. However, Wakefield had no evidence at all to support his claim, and there were many, many pieces of evidence for the safety of the vaccine. But lots of parents became scared and didn't want their children to be vaccinated.

Hundreds of journalists and scientists spent years investigating Wakefield. That's how we know that much of his story is untrue and that he had his own reasons for telling it. Lawyers who were preparing a lawsuit against the vaccine makers had offered a significant amount of money for proof of the side effects. He was also developing another vaccine that could make him a lot of money. And he'd made up pieces of his research, so that it was more in line with the story about the side effects.

Following a lawsuit, Wakefield was no longer allowed to work as a doctor. His stories had done a lot of damage, and they continue to cause harm. In the United Kingdom and the United States, the

number of vaccinated children fell sharply, and the number of children who caught the measles rose. People went on sharing Wakefield's story online. Anti-vaxxers still use the connection between vaccinations and autism as an argument for not vaccinating. But that connection is nonexistent.

Now you might be thinking: "Hey, hang on a moment...so, why should I believe this Marc ter Horst guy?" Good point. All the information I use comes from scientific sources, and I've also had it checked by various scientists. But yes, Wakefield said that too. And he was caught out when other scientists checked up on him. That's how science works. Theories are constantly being adjusted and corrected. New questions are always coming up, for which scientists try to find answers. In this book, I've tried to present the current state of scientific knowledge. And if you doubt the information, you can always check it.

TRUE OR FALSE?

Vaccines come onto the market only after extensive testing with tens of thousands of subjects and an independent evaluation by medical authorities like the FDA (the U.S. Food and Drug Administration). But all it takes for claims about vaccines to show up all over the internet is for someone to have heard a rumor or watched a video. So, we should check a few things.

"Vaccines aren't necessary"
That might seem true, because you rarely see anyone these days with a deformity caused by polio or a face covered with measles. Many viruses we were once terrified of have been significantly reduced or even completely eradicated. Vaccines have played a part in that. But viruses can also hide in, say, a mosquito, a human being, or a pig. If we vaccinate less, then they can come back.

"Vaccines don't work"
Some people who receive the vaccination still get sick, but the disease is usually a lot less serious. There are no vaccines that protect everyone 100 percent of the time. But even a vaccine that's only 70 percent effective is still preventing a lot of people from getting sick—something that benefits both vaccinated and unvaccinated people. So, in fact, a vaccine always works. The more people who receive it, the better. And that goes for the anti-vaxxers, too.

"There are dangerous substances in vaccines"
Besides bit of virus, vaccines also contain ingredients like aluminum and formaldehyde that help the vaccine work better. But these are in such incredibly small amounts that there's nothing to be concerned about—you drink more aluminum in tap water and eat more formaldehyde in a pear.

"Diseases are needed to make your body stronger"
That's right. Vaccines make use of this fact, too: they make you a little bit sick, so that you can handle the real disease. And, of course, it's not true that after a few vaccines you won't ever get sick again. There are still thousands of diseases out there that can make your body stronger. Lucky you!

"God has a purpose with diseases"

This is a hard one to check, but it's what some religious people believe. For this reason, they don't want to be vaccinated and, as a result, outbreaks of infectious diseases often occur in towns and neighborhoods that are home to certain religious communities. However, there are also religious people who say: "Maybe God also has a purpose with vaccines. And besides, we make dikes and levees to stop flooding, don't we? And floods are an act of God, too!" And that's why they decide to get vaccinated.

"Vaccines have side effects"

That's right. But most side effects are mild and just prove that the vaccine works: the immune system has noticed the vaccine and is making antibodies. That can give you a fever or some pain. Worse side effects are more rare, so the risk of having them is much less significant than the misery caused by diseases you could get if you stay unvaccinated.

"We don't know anything about the long-term side effects"

With new vaccines, there's always a bit of tension. But the good thing about most vaccines is that you only have them once or twice, unlike most medicines. A vaccine is a boost for your immune system—and that's that. So, side effects nearly always occur right away and not years later. You can also see this by considering vaccines that have been around for much longer.

"Vaccines cause autism"

Okay, one last time: this has been researched so many times, and it is totally unproven. Just one more study to draw a line under the subject for good: in Denmark, 650,000 children were tracked over a period of ten years. There were no more cases of autism in the group with the MMR vaccine than in the group without. So, there you have it.

LOUIS PASTEUR

GUINEA PIGS

On a summer day in 1885, nine-year-old Joseph Meister was bitten fourteen times on his hands and legs by a dog with rabies. His mother was desperate because rabies in those days was nearly always fatal. She took Joseph to the children's hospital in Paris and asked the famous chemist and biologist Louis Pasteur if there was anything he could do to help. Pasteur had been working for some time on a vaccine against rabies. (If you're upset by animal testing, maybe you should look the other way for the next few lines.)

In his research, Pasteur injected the rabies virus into a rabbit's brain and watched what happened. Then he took some virus from that rabbit and injected it into the next rabbit. This happened a hundred times, and every time it weakened the

strength of the virus, until the last rabbit was only a little bit sick. Next, Pasteur took some tissue with the virus from that rabbit's spine and dried it. The virus was so weakened now that it could no longer do any harm, but it was still strong enough to kick the immune system into action: now Pasteur had a vaccine. Pasteur tried it out on rabid dogs—and some of them recovered. Rabies is one of the few diseases for which you can also give the vaccine after infection. Now all he needed was a guinea pig—in this case, that means a human test subject.

On July 6, 1885, two days after being bitten, Joseph Meister was given his first injection. For the next ten days, he received at least one shot every day, each time with a slightly stronger vaccine. Joseph didn't develop any symptoms—not from the virus in the vaccine and not from the dog bites. When Pasteur examined him months later, the boy

JOSEPH MEISTER

was perfectly healthy. It made some people question whether he had actually been infected with the virus in the first place. But Louis Pasteur was the big hero, in any case, and it was proven afterward that his vaccine really did work. It has since been further improved, and it saves hundreds of thousands of human lives every year.

After his death, it emerged that Pasteur didn't have a medical license. He had secretly done tests on humans and also cheated with his animal experiments. That really wouldn't be possible these days. The development of vaccines has to follow extremely strict rules. First, the vaccine is tested on subjects such as mice, rats, and monkeys. Strict rules also apply to these tests, and you're not allowed to use laboratory animals if it's possible to do the testing without them. Only the vaccines that are proven safe go through to the next set of trials, using human guinea pigs. These trials may differ slightly according to the vaccine, but typically the four phases look like this:

In Phase 1 a few dozen young and healthy volunteers receive increasing amounts of the vaccine. This is how to discover what dose of the vaccine works and is safe for humans.

In Phase 2 a few hundred test subjects get the vaccine. This might include trials with children and older people, depending on the targeted virus. The researchers study the efficacy, the side effects, and, for vaccines requiring more than one dose, what the best timing for the doses is.

Phase 3 involves thousands of volunteers. As with drug tests, the scientists randomly divide the subjects into two groups. One group is given the vaccine, while the other receives a placebo: a fake vaccine. No one knows who is getting which shot, so no one can unknowingly influence the results. This is called a double-blind randomized placebo-controlled trial. (That's a bit of a mouthful!) And then it's a matter of waiting until enough people get sick to see if there's a difference between one group and the other.

With most diseases, this takes years. But in 2020, COVID was so widespread that the trials moved quickly. In one experiment, 44,000 people took part during this phase. Within a couple of months, 178 had caught COVID: 9 with the real vaccine and 169 with the placebo. With a result that clear, you can move on and report it to the medical authorities, an independent group of experts who check that the research has been carried out properly and that the results are correct. The vaccine can be released onto the market only with their approval.

During Phase 4 the manufacturers have to keep a close eye on the efficacy and safety of their vaccine. Now that millions of people have received it, more side effects will naturally emerge—for example, among people who are taking other medications. Doctors and pharmacists have to report these reactions to a public health organization that collects information on side effects. You can also report a side effect yourself, and reports will be tallied and possibly investigated to see which side effects are most common. This allows scientists to mention extra side effects on the information leaflet and to adapt the vaccination—or, in extreme cases, to put a stop to the program.

RUNNING WITH THE RED QUEEN

Dear Lappie,

Doesn't a year fly past?! It's nearly twelve months since you last came to see us for your vaccination. And we want to make sure that you're protected and can play with the other rabbits, so will you come see us again soon for your customized vaccination advice and your annual health check?

I recently came across this message for our rabbit among my old emails. As we no longer have a lawn full of juicy grass, Lappie moved house two years ago, together with her faithful companion, Rob. Now they can have fun again, digging and munching away. And they should still be getting a message from the vet every year. Because rabbits are supposed to get vaccinated against myxomatosis every year. It's a sort of pox for rabbits. Infected rabbits don't usually survive myxomatosis. So, it's a good thing the vet remembers to check in on them every year.

LAPPIE

Myxomatosis is a disease that originally occurred only in the Americas. The rabbits there were used to it, so it didn't cause many problems for them. But in 1950, someone came up with the idea of taking the virus to Australia because that country had a huge rabbit infestation. Those rabbits weren't used to the virus, so masses of them died. More than 99 percent of the rabbits who became infected died of the disease.

The rabbits who survived were immune, and so the virus adapted: it mutated. There was another reason to mutate: the rabbits had all died so

quickly that they hardly had time to infect any other rabbits. The virus would have preferred them to run around with the infection for a while before they dropped dead. So, gradually, a weaker virus developed that made the rabbits sick but was less deadly.

Rabbits and viruses are engaged in an endless arms race. They constantly have to react to each other's moves. This is true of all species—including humans, and how we use vaccines. Some viruses mutate so quickly that we have to keep adapting the vaccines. Twice a year, the World Health Organization decides what the vaccine for the next flu season should be: once for winter in the southern hemisphere, and once for winter in the northern hemisphere. The flu virus constantly adapts to immunity among humans, and that immunity is always changing because we either use vaccines or we catch the flu and get protection. Because it's so hard to predict exactly what the virus is going to be like this winter, the flu vaccine ends up protecting people in only about half of the cases.

Biologists call this "running with the Red Queen," after a scene in *Alice Through the Looking-Glass*. Alice runs with the Red Queen but realizes that they're not going forward. The Queen explains: "Now, here, you see, it takes all the running you can do, to keep in the same place." In other words, if we don't keep reacting to the viruses, we'll lose.

START

6

IN SEARCH OF THE SOURCE

Vaccines can prevent you from getting sick. But wouldn't it be much better to fix things so that vaccines aren't even needed? That would mean finding a way to stop harmful viruses from making the leap to human beings. But where and why do they make that jump? These are questions that take virologists to all corners of the world. For example, to the forests of Africa, as you can read in the Virus Story.

After that you can discover...
• how a letter changed into a number
• why bats can't help it
• why chickens sometimes have lockdowns
• how fake news helps viruses
• which four letters you use to write DNA
• how you can help to prevent virus outbreaks

In short: How virus outbreaks happen and what we can do about them.

THE BAT TREE

KEEP AWAY FROM BATS, MONKEYS, AND DEAD ANIMALS. DON'T TOUCH ANY PEOPLE WITH SYMPTOMS SUCH AS A HIGH FEVER, RED EYES, AND VOMITING. WASH YOUR HANDS REGULARLY WITH CLEAN WATER AND SOAP.

In some African countries, like Liberia, Guinea, and the Democratic Republic of the Congo, you can see posters like this on the roadside. They're warnings that are designed to prevent the spread of Ebola virus. Other posters also say:

SEND PEOPLE WITH EBOLA TO THE EBOLA CLINICS. PROMPT TREATMENT INCREASES THE CHANCE OF SURVIVAL.

These Ebola clinics consist of a number of tents that are quickly put up near a place where an outbreak occurs. But the system there has been well thought out. The confirmed cases of Ebola are separated from the suspected cases and from the staff tents. There are double fences between the different sections, with a wide gap between them, so patients can't infect one another. Doctors and nurses always follow a fixed route through the camp, from the least likely cases to the certain cases, in the high-risk zone. In this way, they can't transmit the virus to people who don't already have it.

Before you enter the high-risk zone, you have to spend about a quarter of an hour putting on protective clothing: rubber boots, plastic coveralls, a sturdy apron, double gloves, a hood over your head and shoulders, and something like ski goggles to cover the last bit of exposed skin. Special assistants help you to get dressed. They check all the seams, and they tape down the zippers and the ends of the gloves. You can't stay in the high-risk zone for longer than an hour because working in those hot suits is extremely tiring. You always go in with someone else so you can keep an eye on how well the other person is coping and whether they have any gaps or tears in their protective gear. Once you're inside, you examine and take care of the patients. One little splash of blood, spit, sweat, or vomit is enough to transmit the virus.

Ebola is a rare and highly contagious disease that occasionally occurs in sub-Saharan Africa. Only half of the people who catch the disease survive. For the first week, Ebola is like flu, but it can soon become more severe, with pain and bleeding in various parts of the body. People quickly become sick with the disease, so it's unable to spread easily—if you're knocked out by Ebola, you're not likely to board a plane.

But what if a variant developed that could spread more quickly? That's why scientists are doing everything they can to get to the bottom of this disease.

It's not that easy, though. Ebola appears in a particular area, claims some victims, and disappears again, only to pop up somewhere else months or years later. Where has the virus been in the meantime? Since the very first outbreak, scientists have been looking for a species—or perhaps several species—in which the virus hides between epidemics. They call this species the reservoir.

The first two known outbreaks of Ebola occurred in 1976, in the Democratic Republic of the Congo and Sudan. The American virologist Karl Johnson traveled with a team to the affected area in the Democratic Republic of the Congo to search for the source of the Ebola virus. He examined hundreds of animals: mosquitoes, mice, rats, cows, pigs, monkeys, bats ... But none of them was carrying the Ebola virus, or antibodies that indicated they'd already been infected by it. Three years later, they searched in other villages in the surrounding forests. But again: no sign of Ebola.

After the first few outbreaks, it was fifteen years before Ebola reappeared. Researchers had not discovered many leads in the meantime. You only know that the virus is around when there are human victims of Ebola.

In January 1995, a farmer in the Democratic Republic of the Congo died of Ebola. He infected his family and friends, and through one of them the virus ended up in the hospital in the nearby city of Kikwit, five miles (eight kilometers) away. Within six months, 250 people died, including 60 members of hospital staff. An international team rushed to the scene. Starting at the property of the deceased farmer, they caught thousands of animals of all shapes and sizes. They took blood and tissue from each of the animals and transported it to a high-security lab in South Africa. Wearing strong, airtight suits, special members of staff inspected the samples. This was a very dangerous job, as any sample might contain the dreaded virus. But no—once again they found nothing.

By that point, it had been noted that dead gorillas and chimpanzees had been found during nearly every outbreak. Were they transmitting the virus to people? That was a possibility. People in those areas often eat bushmeat: meat from the jungle. If you cook it properly, destroying any viruses or bacteria with high heat, it won't do you any harm. But when you're preparing the meat, it's still raw and you can easily become infected. Were the apes a reservoir for Ebola? Probably not. They were found dead, and the reservoir is nearly always a species that isn't badly affected by the virus, so that it can quietly multiply without killing its host.

After 2001, there were a number of small outbreaks in the Democratic Republic of the Congo. These all seemed to start with a hunter who found a dead or sick animal: generally apes, but sometimes porcupines or small antelopes. The French virologist Eric Leroy investigated hundreds of the animals—and this time he found something. Sixteen bats had Ebola antibodies

Two-year-old Emile Ouamouno was one of those children. In December 2013, he had a high fever, diarrhea, and bleeding. Four days later he was dead. In the following weeks, his sister, mother, and grandmother died of Ebola. And in the three years after that, more than 11,000 people passed away. Emile was probably at the beginning of the biggest Ebola outbreak ever.

Was Emile bitten by a bat? Did he get bat poop on his hands and then accidentally wipe it on his eye or nose? Or did he eat a bat that wasn't properly cooked? We'll never know. Fabian Leendertz's team did figure out which species of bat lived in the tree, though: the Angolan free-tailed bat, one of the species in which Ebola antibodies had previously been found.

in their blood. In thirteen other bats he found pieces of Ebola RNA. These were indications that these bats could be the hiding place for Ebola, but they didn't amount to proof. For that, he would have to catch the virus in the act.

Then Ebola broke out in West Africa in 2013 more than 1,800 miles (3,000 kilometers) from the usual risk zone. Many people live in that region and, with lots of cars traveling between villages and towns, it was easy for the virus to spread. The German epidemiologist Fabian Leendertz and his team soon arrived to investigate. This time there were no dead apes or other animals that could be suspected of infection. But then Leendertz heard about the bat tree in the village of Méliandou, a gigantic hollow tree that children often played in. There were hundreds of small bats living in the tree. The children caught them, skewered them on sticks, like marshmallows, and roasted them over fires.

Despite all the research, we still don't know much about Ebola. Probably one or just a few species of bat are the reservoir for the virus. Occasionally a bat infects a chimpanzee, a gorilla, or an antelope. If a person comes into contact with the contaminated meat or with an infected bat, they can become infected, too. With serious consequences. The good news is that there's now a vaccine against Ebola. However, it can be difficult to transport the vaccine to remote regions, and to convince people that the vaccine can protect them.

Wasn't me!

The E B O L A R I V E R

PATIENT ZERO

If you look at the Ebola virus using an electron microscope, you'll see a twisty string that's kind of tangled up with itself. The virus is named after the Ebola, a river that twists and turns almost as much as a tangled piece of string as it meanders through the forests of the Democratic Republic of the Congo. The Ebola River is not far from the village of Yambuku, where one of the first outbreaks of the virus occurred, in 1976. The Belgian microbiologist Peter Piot chose not to name the virus after the village because that would give Yambuku a bad name.

Naming viruses can be tricky. Think about it—would you rather swim in the Ebola or in the Mississippi? That's why the Mexican government wasn't very happy in 2009 when everyone started talking about the "Mexican flu." The pandemic

had indeed begun in Mexico, but Mexico thought "swine flu" was a better name, as the virus probably came from pigs. Other people objected to that name. Pig farmers were afraid no one would want their meat anymore. And Jews and Muslims found the name offensive because pigs are unclean in their religions.

So, since 2015, the World Health Organization has had rules in place for naming. Viruses can no longer be named after animals or places, for example. Some people don't care about the rules, though. In 2020, the American president Donald Trump kept calling the coronavirus the "China virus," just because it came from there, or so he said. Millions of Chinese people all over the world have been discriminated against as a result—as if they were all infectious or guilty.

In Méliandou, even years after Ebola, they're still having problems because of such prejudices. The village is known as the starting point of the biggest Ebola outbreak ever, but the place has been free of Ebola for years now. People used to come from all around to buy rice, corn, and bananas in the village. But now custmers stay away, out of fear or superstition. This is an extra blow for this village, where many people who were already poor lost family members to Ebola, and now make even less money than before. And all because Emile Ouamouno went to play by the bat tree. As the epidemic probably started with him, Emile is considered the Patient Zero of this outbreak of Ebola. That's what we call the first person to become infected with a virus. Which is a bit weird, because they should, of course, be Patient One. But it gets even weirder than that.

PATIENT
ZERO

The first person ever to be known as Patient Zero was not a Patient Zero at all. It was Gaëtan Dugas, a Canadian flight attendant who took part in an AIDS study in California in 1984. As his job involved a lot of flying, he often had to spend the night in California, and he had sexual contact with a lot of men. Because he came from outside of California, he was given the designation of "Patient O" in the study, with "O" meaning "outside of California." Someone mistook the letter for a number—and from then on Gaëtan Dugas was Patient Zero. This had serious consequences. Articles, movies, and a book came out about "the man who brought AIDS to the United States." But in 2016, a study showed that Gaëtan was definitely not the first person to become infected with HIV, the virus that causes AIDS.

PATIENT
O

ON THE EDGE OF THE FOREST

Many viruses that jump to humans come from bats. But does that mean bats are the bad guys? Not really. It's just that there are lots and lots of species of bats. Around 20 percent of the approximately 7,000 known species of mammals are bats. That's about 1,400 bat species in total. All those species have their own population of viruses. But so do ducks, warthogs, and squirrels. Viruses can hide in one of these reservoirs for thousands of years, endlessly multiplying, before they make the leap to a human being, sometimes by way of another animal, such as a chimpanzee, a mink, or a pangolin. But that jump is never actually the bat's idea. It really isn't the case that bats wake up at night, hanging from their branches, and think: *I know! I'm going to go cough in a human's face so I can pass on my virus!* Most jumps are the result of human interventions in nature. Yes, that's right: we have ourselves to blame for most virus outbreaks.

Scientists have studied satellite images of twenty-seven areas where Ebola broke out. In twenty-five of those regions, some of the surrounding forest had recently been cut down: to build roads, to grow crops, or simply to sell the wood. Those forests are the animals' territory. Of course. They're home to noisy monkeys, poisonous frogs, intricate insects, colorful birds, shy rodents, and many species no human has ever seen.

Inside those animals, viruses are lurking. Viruses that are not likely to come into contact with human beings. But if you start cutting down trees, that changes things. Look at that farmer from the village near Kikwit. When you start cutting down trees, animals have less and less habitat. A tree that was deep in the forest is suddenly on the edge of the forest. Animals from a chopped-down tree move to a tree in the middle of the village. And the viruses move with them. As a result, they get closer and closer to people.

But people also get closer and closer to the viruses: for example, by hunting apes, pangolins, and other animals from the forest. This meat is an important source of protein for many people in these regions. But all it takes is for the cook to cut himself with a knife that has just sliced through a piece of raw meat—and that's enough for a virus to make the jump.

More and more people are eating bushmeat. Rich people in big cities will pay a lot of money for bushmeat, particularly from rare animals, like gorillas. So more roads are built to make it easier for hunters to get deep into the forest, which leads to deforestation, and that threatens biodiversity (the number of plant and animal species in an area). Also, traffickers smuggle truckloads of meat to cities all over the world. And the viruses go along for the ride.

So, that's another problem we've brought upon ourselves. Our planet is home to more and more people, we're living closer and closer together, and we're traveling more and more. We're making life very easy for the viruses. Just take a look at Ebola. Between 1976 and 2014, there were roughly twenty outbreaks, nearly all of which were contained within a few weeks and claimed a few hundred lives at most. Most were in remote regions where not many people lived. Then the outbreak in West Africa happened, and it lasted two and a half years, from 2014 to 2016, and took more than 11,000 lives. There are all kinds of reasons for this, but it certainly made a difference that, compared to previous outbreaks, this one occurred in a much more densely populated area with better roads.

Now you might be thinking: obviously they shouldn't cut the trees down. But deforestation often takes place for products that you and I use. Trees are cut down to create palm plantations for the palm oil that's in our chips, chocolate, and shampoo. Trees are cut down so that people can extract rare metals from the ground that are necessary for your phone and gaming computer. And trees are cut down to grow soy to feed our cows. So, maybe it's unrealistic to think that those forests can stay untouched, but...
it would be good if people bought fewer products containing palm oil, made do with their old phones and computers for longer, and ate less meat and other animal products.

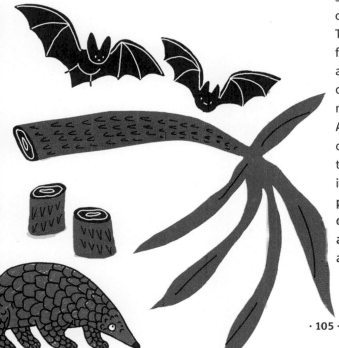

ALL TOGETHER NOW

Dogs watch wide-eyed from their cages, waiting to see who's going to take them. Turtles crawl over one another in a crate that's sealed up with wire mesh. A woman in a plastic apron and gloves chops off a duck's head. Welcome to the animal market in Wuhan. Many of the animals for sale are still alive. Most of the customers here like their meat to be fresh, so the animals aren't slaughtered until they're sold. But you can also buy dried bat wings here, or pungent snake soup, or stir-fried civet cat.

On January 1, 2020, the live-animal market in Wuhan was closed down. The new coronavirus had just been discovered, and more than half of the people infected at the time had recently visited that market. That immediately made the market look suspicious. There were so many animals, from all parts of nature, all packed in close together, anxious and stressed and therefore more susceptible to sickness. The gutters were full of mud, blood, slaughter waste, and bird droppings; now and then a shoe would step into it and carry the muck to the other side of the market. It must have been like an amusement park for viruses.

The coronavirus could have made the jump somewhere else. Maybe there was a trader at the market who had caught the virus in another place and then infected his customers by coughing and sneezing. Nevertheless, the fact remains that markets like the one in Wuhan are dangerous breeding grounds for viruses. An animal market probably played an important role in the development of SARS, too. For this reason, lots of people are calling for live-animal markets to be banned—and let's not forget animal welfare and the trade in endangered species, of course. However, a lot of those people who are calling for change probably don't live that far from another breeding ground for viruses. Huge sheds full of chickens, pigs, or goats might not be quite so much of an amusement park for viruses as the live-animal market in Wuhan, but a virus can still have plenty of fun there. And so can bacteria, by the way.

In spring 2007, a lot of patients in Herpen, a small town in the Netherlands, consulted their doctor, all suffering from a strange sort of flu. They were examined and found to be infected with Q fever, a disease that causes miscarriages in goats. The fever had taken hold in a large goat farm outside the village, and the bacteria had blown into the village on the wind. Luckily, the disease hardly ever passes from person to person, but it does make the jump from animals to humans. That was how the bacteria also reached other places

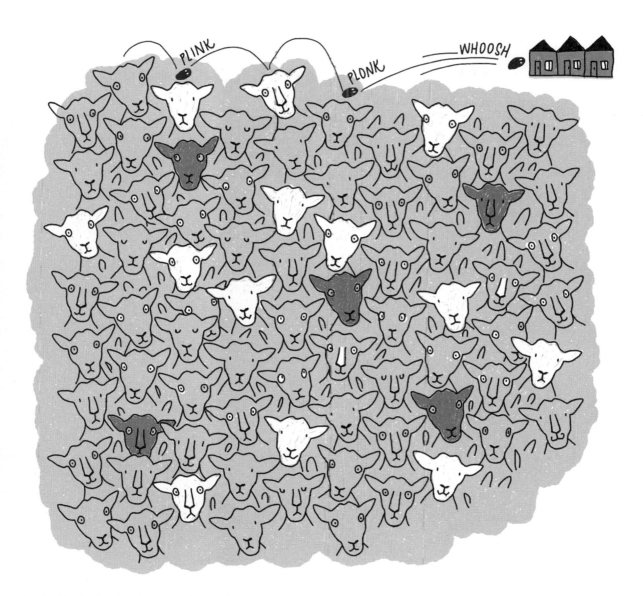

PLINK

PLONK

WHOOSH

in the Netherlands. At least ninety-five people died, and hundreds more suffered from fatigue for years. When the severity of the situation became clear, the government decided to cull more than 60,000 sheep and goats. To kill them, in other words. Animal to human transmission can happen anywhere animals are raised in factory farms, it seems. There's a theory that the virus we learned not to call "the Mexican flu" actually originated in factory farms in the United States.

Culling also happens regularly with chickens and other birds when bird flu breaks out. A bit of infected bird poop on a chicken farmer's shoe can be all it takes to bring bird flu into a shed. And there can be more than 100,000 chickens, ducks, or turkeys in one of these sheds. They all have to be culled, and the birds in the surrounding area go into a sort of chicken lockdown. Because bird flu is very infectious. The animals can also infect humans, but usually that's not dangerous. There is a small chance, though, that bird flu will mutate and jump from human to human. That could be the beginning of a dangerous pandemic. It's how the 1918 flu started...

CAUGHT: VIRUS SPREADS FAKE NEWS!!!

Sometimes you can easily recognize fake news by the sensational headline and the line of exclamation points it comes with. But often it's packaged in the form of a slick video or a professional-looking article. It seems official—and that's exactly what conspiracy theorists want. Conspiracy theorists are people who reject the most obvious and commonly accepted explanation for events and instead go looking for a darker version, one that generally involves a truth that others are supposedly conspiring to keep from the general public.

Some conspiracy theorists think, for example, that the coronavirus is the result of the construction of 5G cell towers. They might believe that viruses don't even exist, or that they're just waste products from human cells. Some seem sure that viruses can't infect other people. Others have decided that if we're still not 100 percent sure where the coronavirus originated, then it obviously must have escaped from a laboratory where scientists were designing biological weapons. Conspiracy theorists might tell you that billionaire Bill Gates spread the coronavirus so he could get even richer selling everyone a vaccine, and that maybe the vaccine contains a microchip that will allow him to track everyone. I could fill an entire page with conspiracy theories.

In most parts of the world, people are allowed to say what they think. But that doesn't mean that what someone says is necessarily true. Without evidence, these are just opinions, not facts. Journalists and scientists carry out extensive research before they make any claims, and everyone is free to check their theories and possibly disagree. But no one has ever proved that the coronavirus comes from 5G, or that there's a microchip in vaccines.

Conspiracy theorists may claim that they have proof. They often say they've done extensive research too. But when it comes to viruses, it's safe to assume that virologists and epidemiologists have spent a lot longer and taken a much more scientific approach to investigating the subject than, say, a podcaster, a radio host, or a professor from an entirely different scientific field. That's why it's always a good idea to google the name of the person who made the website you're reading or the video you're watching. Then you'll see what their real area of expertise is. Sometimes you'll discover that someone else has already helpfully investigated whether that person is talking nonsense or not. And, with a little detective work, you can often find out *why* someone is spreading that nonsense.

Sometimes it's just a matter of self-interest. Conspiracy theorists say things that support their opinions or fill their wallets. For example, you'll find most stories about dangerous vaccines on sites for anti-vaxxers. On websites that blame 5G, you'll be able to buy a card that "protects you against unnatural radiation everywhere" for "a bargain price." Don't forget that some people have political or economic reasons for blaming other countries for problems that affect all of us. And enemies of China are always on the look-out for excuses to blame the Chinese for... well, pretty much anything.

For many people, conspiracies are primarily an attempt to get a handle on something that's dangerous and feels very complicated. You've almost finished this book now, and you know that the world of viruses isn't easy to understand. But conspiracy theorists often prefer to go for an explanation that's less accurate but easier to grasp. People used to blame epidemics on the position of the planets or the wrath of God. Nowadays they're more likely to think of 5G or Bill Gates.

BILL GATES

Conspiracy theorists who believe that a virus doesn't exist or that it's not dangerous probably think the measures taken against it are nonsense as well. As a result, there's a large group of people who happily go on partying and shaking hands at times when they really shouldn't. And meanwhile the virus is chuckling away to itself. You could almost think it made up the conspiracy theories itself, so that it could keep on doing its own thing. That's why it's vital to prevent the spread of fake news as much as possible.

AND NOW FOR THE GOOD NEWS

The right order

Just a few weeks after the first sick person reported to the hospital, virologists were able to unmask the new coronavirus. They did this with sequencing, a clever technique for reading the DNA or RNA of a virus. This used to be a huge job, which you needed a big machine for. These days it can be done much faster, with a machine the size of a phone. Sequencing is quite a complicated process, but it comes down to putting the strands of DNA or RNA through a device that reads their code. The code consists of four letters: A, C, G, and T (for DNA), or A, C, G, and U (for RNA). The order that those letters appear in determines the characteristics of the virus and forms a sort of fingerprint. Sequencing the coronavirus involved unraveling about 30,000 letters, more than all the letters in Chapter 6.

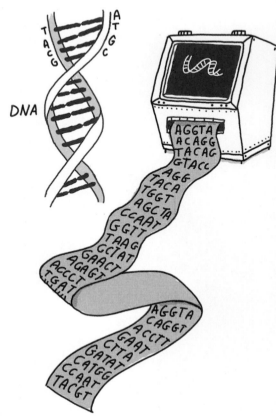

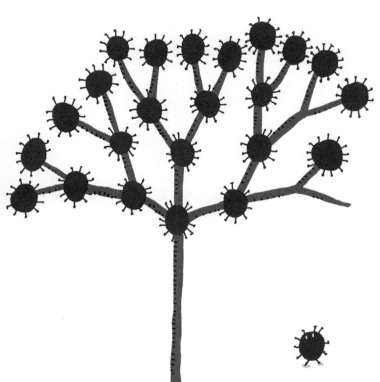

Tracking down mutations

When viruses make copying errors, the code of their DNA or RNA changes. The more these codes are alike, the closer they are to the point of origin of the virus particles. By doing a lot of testing and sequencing, we can make an entire family tree of the virus, and we can quickly notice if a dangerous mutation appears. It was sequencing that allowed scientists to establish that the coronavirus must have made the jump from animals to humans in early December 2019.

Rapid vaccines

By quickly working out the code of the coronavirus, vaccine manufacturers were able to start designing a vaccine right away. It also helped that they were able to build on their experience with the SARS vaccine. At the start of the pandemic, the World Health Organization expected that it would be at least eighteen months before a vaccine against the coronavirus was available. But thanks to a flying start, modern technology, and international collaboration, it was less than a year before the first approved vaccine was injected into someone's arm.

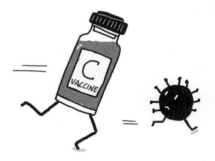

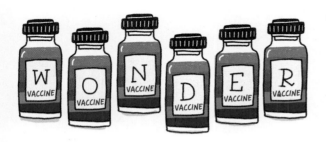

More vaccines

The new technique of making vaccines with synthetic RNA appears to have been a resounding success. Perhaps it will also finally enable scientists to create a vaccine that can deal with all forms of flu in one go. And maybe it will be possible to develop a vaccine against HIV, something that scientists have been trying to do for forty years.

Good intentions

Even at the beginning of the pandemic, people were already saying that they didn't want to go back to the way things were before. And we're not talking about shaking hands and hugging and kissing when we meet one another. People want to work from home more and to travel—or at least to fly—less. They want to live in a more sustainable way by, for example, eating less meat and not buying products that contain palm oil. And lots of many countries want to ban the trade in wild animals and improve their health care system.

Down to work

The coronavirus pandemic has made it clear to everyone that infectious diseases can take us by surprise. Now is the time to combat future pandemics—for example, by setting up major projects against deforestation and the wildlife trade. That will cost a lot of money, but scientists have calculated that future pandemics will cost even more. There are also projects that involve better prediction of where a disease will break out and what the disease will look like. It might involve testing suspicious animals for viruses, and getting people to use an app to report where they see virus carriers like tiger mosquitoes. That way, everyone can help to prevent new pandemics.

CHEESE

WHOOWHOOWHOO!!!

We are all living in a world of viruses. That's always been the case, but recently it's become very clear. You could see the pandemic as an alarm signal: "Wake up, world! Don't forget about us!" What Ebola said was: *beepbeepbeep!* What SARS said was: *BEEPBEEPBEEP!* And what COVID is saying is: *WHOOwhooWHOO!!!*

According to scientists, we can expect more virus outbreaks in the years to come. That's the price we pay for our modern way of life. More and more people are coming into the world, and they all have to eat. Forests are chopped down for agriculture. More and more wild animals are killed for meat, and more and more animals are kept in captivity. Big cities are built for humans.

So humans are living closer together—and also closer to animals. This makes it easier for animal diseases to make the jump to humans. By traveling more and faster, we also help diseases to spread across the world at lightning speed. Airplanes, cars, and factories release lots of greenhouse gases into the air. This warms the Earth and gives mosquitoes and other creatures more opportunity to spread diseases. What a mess.

Fortunately, the modern age has also brought a lot of good things. Thanks to science, people are on average living longer, healthier lives. Thanks to the internet, we're able to share knowledge swiftly. We have techniques that allow us to recognize viruses rapidly. Using medical technology, we can quickly create vaccines, and if a virus changes, we can adapt the vaccines to match. We are building on the work of scientists such as Antonie van Leeuwenhoek, John Snow, and Louis Pasteur. We have experience with SARS, Ebola, and now COVID. In short, we have something that viruses don't have: brains. If we're smart, we'll use those brains to prevent future virus outbreaks.

We can reduce the likelihood of pandemics by cutting down fewer trees, eating less meat, and traveling less. Every outbreak we prevent can spare us a lot of misery, while saving millions of lives and also tons of money. In that respect, prevention works even better than vaccines.

The good news is that measures of this kind also help to combat global climate change, another problem of our age. So, we can solve two problems in one go. It's just too bad that the *WHOOwhooWHOO!!!* hasn't woken up everyone. Maybe it will help if you pass on the information in this book to the people around you. Let's hope it spreads—like a virus!

Thank You

Early in the first lockdown, I rode my bike to the bookstore. I sanitized my hands and headed straight for a book that I was very curious about: *Spillover*, by the American writer David Quammen. "Spillover" is the word for diseases jumping from animals to humans. I didn't know much about the subject, but 592 pages later, I was under the spell of bacteria and viruses.

The subject kept bubbling away in the back of my mind as I closely followed the news about the pandemic every day. I thought: *my fellow authors are probably all writing children's books about viruses now*. But my editor, Marleen Louter, told me it was fewer than I thought. That was really when I knew: I had to write Snot, Sneezes, and Super-Spreaders, and Wendy had to do the illustrations.

A little boldly, I looked up the email address of Marion Koopmans. As a member of the World Health Organization and professor of virology at the Erasmus University Rotterdam, she was obviously at the top of the list of experts I wanted to ask to read what I wrote. The following day, I was literally jumping and down with joy: Maaike van Zuilen emailed me on behalf of Marion Koopmans to say that she'd be happy to help.

As the virus retreated and the world started to open up again, I read all about immunity, Ebola, and previous pandemics. After the summer vacation, I started to work on the book almost without interruption. Just after Children's Book Week, in October 2020, a letter arrived from the Dutch Foundation for Literature to say that my application for a subsidy had been approved. That meant that not only could I work without interruption, I could also work without financial worries. I drove to Huisseling and, from a safe distance, I sat at the kitchen table with Jesper, Veronique, and Ulrieke Kocken and interviewed them about their grandfather.

I sent the first chapters to my beta readers. During the busiest time of their lives, Marion Koopmans and Maaike van Zuilen found time to check the text for virological accuracy. They were helped by their colleagues Thijs Kuiken, Rik de Swart, Rob Gruters, and Bas Oude Munnink. Mads, Rixt, and Marjolijn Hovius checked that the book was fun and understandable for children. Edzard van der Molen did the same on his own. Coen Klein Douwel tried to give me a refresher course on physics and science. Mark van Heck discovered peculiarities in the text that everyone else had overlooked. And at home on the sofa, I worked through all of Edith's question marks and exclamation points with her until she could put a happy face beside everything.

David, Marleen, Wendy, Marion, Maaike, the Dutch Foundation for Literature, Jesper, Veronique, Ulrieke, Thijs, Rik, Rob, Bas, Mads, Rixt, Marjolijn, Edzard, Coen, Mark, and Edith, thank you! Without you, the world of viruses would have been much less clear and fascinating.

INDEX

This index is like a map, showing you where to find information inside this book. Think of a topic related to viruses, and look for the main heading which matches that topic. For example, the topic tiger mosquitoes is found under the main heading "tiger mosquitoes." All of the main headings are in alphabetical order. After each main heading are page numbers which direct you to where you can learn more information. Page numbers in a range, as in 70–71, means that information is found on both pages 70 *and* 71. Some main headings are also followed up subheadings. So under "humans," you will see subheadings for "as test subjects," "viruses in and on your body," and "viruses jumping from animals to humans." These subheadings can help you narrow your search to a more specific topic. Sometimes similar information is listed under a different main heading. You can find these if you see the words *See* or *See also*, and follow the cross-reference to the other main heading. For example, if you look up "rabbits," you will notice a cross-reference to "arctic hares."